"THE TEACHING
OF READING
IN THE
INTERMEDIATE GRADES"

BROWN

EDUCATION SERIES

Edited by

Lowry W. Harding, Ph.D.
The Ohio State University
Columbus, Ohio

"THE TEACHING
OF READING
IN THE
INTERMEDIATE GRADES"

STANLEY S. STAHL, Jr., Ed.D.
Professor of Education
University of Virginia

LB
1632
.578

WM. C. BROWN   COMPANY   PUBLISHERS
135 SOUTH LOCUST STREET   •   DUBUQUE, IOWA 52003

Manufactured by WM. C. BROWN CO. INC., Dubuque, Iowa
Printed in U. S. A.

Illustrated
by
Carolyn Copp

PREFACE

This book is not designed as an all-inclusive volume covering the entire reading process. There are already many excellent texts on reading which are available if a comprehensive picture is desired. *Teaching in the Intermediate Grades* is intended for students, teachers, principals, supervisors and parents who wish a concise description of what should happen to a child's reading abilities as he reaches that marvelously creative and inquisitive state associated with the intermediate grades. The reader of this book will encounter no panacea for reading programs, nor will he be startled by a critical exposé or biased defense of present practice. He will, however, be permitted a view of reading through a series of processes and will, it is hoped, be stimulated to further study by the discussion questions and reading.

The author is deeply indebted to many of his colleagues who have given of their time and knowledge to assist in many ways. To Evelyn P. Bickham, Principal of the Clark School in Charlottesville, is owed a debt of gratitude for contributing many worthwhile ideas to the manuscript. Of particular note are the inspiration and contribution of Dr. Ullin W. Leavell, founder of the McGuffey Reading Clinic and Director from 1946 to 1959, whose untimely death in 1960 prevented a joint authorship of this book. Many of his lofty guidelines to reading have been incorporated into the text, and it is to his memory that this book is dedicated.

S.S.S.

TABLE OF CONTENTS

CHAPTER   *PAGE*

1. **Introduction**   1
   The Reading Process   2
   The Reading Program   8

2. **The Teaching of Reading at the Fourth Grade Level**   15
   Determining and Establishing Readiness   16
   Reading as a Mental Process   23
   Reading as a Communicative Process   25
   Reading as a Pleasurable Process   34
   Reading as a Process Requiring the Development of Many Skills   35
   Reading as a Means of Cultivating Oral and Written Self-Expression   39

3. **The Teaching of Reading at the Fifth Grade Level**   46
   Planning the Program   46
   Reading as a Mental Process   48
   Reading as a Communicative Process   53
   Reading as a Pleasurable Process   60
   Reading as a Process Requiring the Development of Many Skills   63
   Reading as a Means of Cultivating Oral and Written Self-Expression   66

4. **The Teaching of Reading at the Sixth Grade Level**   73
   Reading as a Mental Process   75
   Reading as a Communicative Process   77

Reading as a Pleasurable Process 81
Reading as a Process Requiring the Development and Perfection of Many Skills 83
Reading as a Means of Cultivating Oral and Written Self-Expression 86

5. **The Remedial Program** 93
Disability in Reading 93
Diagnostic Study 97
Correction of Difficulty 102
Corrective Materials 104

APPENDIX 109
A. Skill Building Materials for Intermediate Grades 109
B. Publishers and Addresses 111

THE TEACHING
OF READING
IN THE
INTERMEDIATE GRADES

CHAPTER 1

INTRODUCTION

Reading   is a   Complex Symbolic Process

All language is symbolic. A writer never writes a meaning itself. He writes only symbols — one or more words — that stand for the meaning which he wishes to convey to the reader. No reader ever sees on the written or printed page the meaning which the writer intends to convey to him. He sees only the symbols which the writer has used to represent his meaning. Thus, written or printed words, phrases, sentences, paragraphs, and punctuation marks are only symbols behind which lie, more or less hidden, the meanings that the writer intends.[1]

If the above statement, which is typical of many others concerning the written word, is studied carefully, the full extent of the complexity of the reading process becomes evident. Scores

---

[1]Paul McKee, *The Teaching of Reading.* New York: Houghton-Mifflin Company, 1948, page 5.

of texts, pamphlets and articles, many based upon extensive research, have been written in an attempt to explain and clarify this process. The average elementary school child, working at his own speed and capabilities, is undergoing and mastering this extremely complex process, a truly remarkable achievement when the possibilities of failure are enumerated.

The Reading Process

The child who is enjoying success at the intermediate level has actually overcome a host of barriers including weaknesses in areas such as environment, physical growth, emotional stability, and intellectual ability, and an extensive set of reading concepts. The ability to read at the intermediate level presupposes an elemental capacity to employ structural and phonetic methods, skill in the immediate recognition of words, a mental set which accommodates itself to purposeful or pleasurable reading activity, an ability to extract meaning from written material with some degree of accuracy and acuity, and at least a fair measure of curiosity. By such mastery, the child would be virtually equipped to educate himself, and if his natural inclinations or only a little conscious other motivation led him to select for himself those reading materials and pursuits which would be most useful to him and most propitious to his development, he might be supplied with ample reading matter and left alone to educate and amuse himself and, incidentally, to increase his reading rate and efficiency. The desire to learn certainly is the indispensable factor at this stage, and if this desire is augmented by good teaching, the optimum outcomes in progress and development are foreseeable. Such a desirable blending of optimums cannot, however, be brought about by wishful thinking and benevolent guidance or by mechanical plodding.

Just as the learning process undergoes great change from the primary to the intermediate grades, so the teaching methods must be altered to meet the changing needs and developing interests of the pupils. Teaching at the primary level is a method-

Children who read more
become men who achieve more

3

ical process. Definite goals must be achieved, and definable methods are instituted to enable their attainment. Maximum effectiveness demands teaching ability and enthusiasm, but measurable results may be attained by attending to the mechanics of the process alone. Not so at the intermediate level. Teaching methods are not so clearly defined. Goals are less the outcome of the actual tasks assigned than of the intrinsic values which grow out of continual and meaningful performance of and dedication to the tasks. Teaching can be considered an exact science at the primary level; at the intermediate level it becomes a fine art. This factor, however, does not exclude all but the talented from attempting to teach the intermediate grades. Fortunately, teaching is an art which can be cultivated by those who harbor an inclination to liberate and challenge young minds and to direct the processes by which they achieve growth and satisfaction.

Content Areas and Reading. History, geography, science, safety, hygiene, grammar and literature become the reading content which formerly was all too-often limited to only the story form. Arithmetic, too, relies increasingly upon reading, albeit a specialized form of reading, for understanding and solution. Emphasis placed upon any of the foregoing elements of curriculum as being independently significant, apart from *reading* as such, is misleading and not justifiable. In the separate curricular emphasis frequently employed with the subject of history, for example, the memorizing of dates may be required. Memorizing dates can in itself be meaningful or meaningless, innocuous or inimically dull. Seldom, if ever, should the aim of reading be to commit certain facts to permanent retention. One of the remarkable characteristics of the human mind is its ability to forget those things which are not vital or pleasant to think upon.

> *"The horror of that moment," the King went on, "I shall never, NEVER forget."*

HISTORY

Literature

SCIENCE

HYGIENE

SAFETY

Grammar:

GEOGRAPHY

NEW MATH

READING

Curricular Areas Supply the Reading Content

*"You will, though," the Queen said, "if you don't make
a memorandum of it."*

LEWIS CARROLL

The aim, then, of reading history is the same as that of reading a story: to familiarize oneself with the content examined
to the extent of comprehending the facts and ideas presented
and enable oneself to answer pertinent and lucid questions concerning the facts or to discuss intelligently or summarize the
content. These comments are intended to provide the teacher
with a background of perspective and not to restrict the teaching of subject matter. Requiring dates and facts to be retained
for a specified period will facilitate the development of certain
reading skills if it is employed rather rarely and with the emphasis and explanation essential to establish meaningfulness.
To know, in relation to the present time, the antiquity of an
event, the origin of an idea, or the life of a hero, may be very
meaningful. Merely to recite the dates of a list of happenings
with no frame of reference is meaningless. To know a time as
a historical era in which people dressed a certain way, believed
certain things, travelled by means of certain forms of transportation, etc., to know that this was about three hundred years ago,
and to have at least a vague appreciation of how long three hundred years are should be a prerequisite to memorizing the dates
of the Revolutionary War.

The photostatic memory is phenomenal, and the dubious skill
of reciting a list of facts, despite the monetary inducement of
certain well-known quiz programs, is an example of the exploita-
tion and not the enrichment of the human mind. The ability
to comprehend meaning, to analyze concepts, to evaluate ideas
against a frame of reference, to classify, to summarize, and
finally to create, is the aim of enrichment. Physical exercises,
properly considered, are not performed primarily for their intrinsic worth but for the general well-being of the body. Mental
exercises, correctly viewed, are not performed as ends in achievement, but as methods of enriching the mind and increasing its
functional use. The reading of history at the intermediate level,

then, prepares the pupil to read the same historical facts with enlightened interest at a more advanced level, to weigh the means against the ends, to compare and evaluate the courses of action and outcomes of different events, eventually to apply the knowledge of hindsight to the problems of the present with logical foresight. Finally, perhaps, it prepares the pupil to read from history the part of the philosophy of man which it reveals to those who read with a broad frame of reference, acquired developmentally and gradually as a result of reading and thinking, thinking and delving — never as a result of the mere retention of names and dates and the paraphernalia of pseudo-knowledge in which small winds drown themselves.

Background for Reading. The increased field of subject matter presented in the intermediate grades, far from being a burden, should provide an opportunity for exploration into many facets of human experience and an increased awareness of the interaction of all areas of study with each other, with life itself, and with one's own personality. Obviously, the pupil will at this stage come into contact with subject matter about which he has never expressed interest and with which he has not had previous experience. The factor of readiness to read therefore becomes of paramount importance and receives a degree of emphasis at least equal to that which it requires at the preparational stages in laying the ground work for the initial teaching of reading.

Pupils who have lived on a diet of sweet little stories about children and pets can not suddenly relish the meaty facts of science, geography, and history, and certainly should not be required to digest them before the appetite is prepared to receive them. Pupils who have had certain experiences on their own will show an immediate readiness for reading related subject matter. The child who has had an aquarium in his home is prepared for certain elementary science studies. The child who has been to the mountains, the ocean, lakes, plains, and caverns, who has had firsthand experience with various forms of transportation, and who appreciates the usefulness, if not the use, of maps, is perhaps ready for geography. Similarly, the child who has long been told or read stories of George Washington, Thomas Jefferson, and Abraham Lincoln, and who has seen pictures of their homes and times, can relate historical facts to the familiar figures, and has a background of readiness in history. There are, however, children from impoverished or indifferent cultural backgrounds who have not been acquainted with the biographical facts of the lives of heroes, who have not travelled, and who have not been challenged to know more about the fascinating activity of an ant hill. There also are children who have been privileged to know much of one but little or none of another. The teacher must be aware of this situation and must not assign or present subject matter which any or all of her pupils are not prepared to receive. Special attention must be given to the problems of *determining and establishing readiness* at each grade level.

The Reading Program

The program of reading instruction at the intermediate level, then, must be concerned with the development of in-depth perception of the meaning behind the printed word, going far beyond the basic skills covered at the primary level. Reading now becomes a series of processes through which the child explores, meditates, enjoys, and creates beyond the mere recall of words. The role of the teacher must reflect this changing pattern, as he now stimulates the reader to a deeper understanding and is no longer the drillmaster insisting upon the mastery of phonetic clues, word recall and the many vital basic steps that must be thoroughly mastered before the reader can move ahead with independence and understanding. These intermediate processes now embrace:

a. Reading as a mental process
b. Reading as a communicative process
c. Reading as a pleasurable process

d. Reading as a process requiring the cultivation of many skills

e. Reading as a process facilitating oral and written self-expression

Reading as a mental process attains a loftier significance as exploratory experience in more areas of learning equips the child to read more critically and to bring more types of knowledge to each new reading experience, thereby making possible initial strides in the cultivation of discrimination, judgment, and logical and comparative reasoning.

Reading as a communicative process likewise achieves status as the child becomes more effective in receiving ideas or facts against a wider background of information and more firm opinions, and projecting them upon the screen of total experience for scrutiny and evaluation. (This is the age group that begins to demand truth and has an uncanny ability to "see through" the bluffs, pretensions and half-truths which are sometimes inflicted upon it in the forms of words or persons.)

The *increased* attention to oral reading as a communicative device attains social status as the need to understand and be understood begins to develop. This need is expressed in the intermediate years in the desire for social acceptance. The child seeks identification and unity with his contemporaries and is miserable when he (or his ideas) is (are) rejected. The selection of reading material to share and discuss with interested classmates provides a common background of understanding and experience and becomes a bond between those who give and receive. Later, in the adolescent years, conscious attention of the pupils to concepts in human relations will be a vital factor in their growth and development. Incidental and directed consideration of special social and moral problems at the intermediate level presented through the reading program encourages the establishment of individual principles and criteria for living in and evaluating the social situation.

Reading as a pleasurable process achieves significance as the pupil finds himself equipped to read a wide variety of material with discernment. Hitherto, he has been confined to books and stories for the primary reading levels, necessarily limited in scope because of vocabulary inadequacies and his restriction of interest and experience. The world of interests opening to the child who begins to have an appreciation for science and history enables him to avail himself of the opportunity of reading hundreds of books each year at his level which explain, supplement, entertain, and popularize history and science. He can appreciate firsthand at this level some of the gems of literature, and the possibilities which teacher and parental guidance, reading ability and interest lay open to him are astounding and well worth the tireless efforts directed at motivating him to read, discover and grow.

Reading as a process requiring the cultivation of many skills will receive marked emphasis at this level. At the intermediate level the rules of correct speech and grammar can be understood as well as applied to advantage. Learning rules should be viewed similar to the treatment given to the memorizing of historical dates. No rule (and no date) should be memorized until it is meaningful. A number of rules governing spelling, pronunciation, sentence structure and punctuation can be learned with meaning at the intermediate level because they have been exemplified throughout the primary reading experience. The presentation of the following rule is a case in point:

In words of one syllable ending in e, the first vowel usually is long and the final e is silent.

To make this rule meaningful it is but necessary to present such words as ride, side, made, globe, take, etc., which have long been familiar, to lead pupils to observe that the final e is not heard in any of them and that the first vowel in each of them is long. The pupils with more logical minds are capable of stating the rule inductively, perhaps clumsily, but at least with sufficient intelligence to demonstrate that it is understood.

The teacher can then state the rule in a more polished form and assign an exercise for its application. Any pupil who has followed this process of inductive reasoning and application of the logical conclusion is ready to memorize the rule and to enlist it in the future when he encounters such words as *mute, tripe* and *slake.*

The wording of the rule need not be memorized; it need not be reproduced in the same manner again. The thought or the gist of the rule, however, must be incorporated into the thinking and eventually become a mental habit which is applied without statement as one of the unconscious skills of reading. The teaching of skills by application or by rules and their application promotes reading progress by pinpointing those elements of word and sentence structure (which left alone would become recurring difficulties) and by controlled and concentrated practice, making them familiar and spontaneous responses. It is possible to learn to read without attention to the isolated skills. An intelligent first grade pupil confronted twenty-five times with the initial consonants in twenty-five different words would naturally associate the sound of s with the letter symbol s, although he had been taught the word wholes and not the name nor the sound of the letter s. Similarly, an intelligent third or fourth grade pupil, from frequent experience with the rule given (as it is applied — not stated) might pronounce the word *mete* as a result of his experience with fifty-seven words previously encountered in which the first vowel is long, the final *e* is silent. For the average child, and frequently for the superior pupil, greater independence and confidence result from having had isolated practice with the rule or concept.

Reading as a process facilitating oral and written self-expression has broader application at the intermediate level. This is true because the pupil now has more to say and a larger speaking and writing vocabulary with which to say it. His experiences are meaningful because they are more diverse and at the same time, paradoxically, more unified. He has now arrived at the same time, at a stage in his maturity when he can relate assimilated information and conglomerated experiences, albeit not always correctly or happily, to his own persons, ideas or opinions. He explains things in terms of his own experience with them or his own knowledge of them, however limited these may be. Like the blind men who described the elephant in terms of the particular part of the pachyderm which they touched and saw, the child at this level thus will harbor strong convictions and will exhibit ardent loyalty or strong malice on the basis of his immature but personally convincing experiences and observations.

The child therefore needs not only an opportunity daily, perhaps hourly, to express himself, but also careful guidance from an understanding teacher who views his dedications to fallacy or half-truths as a stage in his developing maturity and not as a field for contention and persuasion. His understanding is broadened as the teacher places herself in his position, looks with his eyes (immaturely but not defectively) and then; by skillful questioning or handling, corrects or diminishes the error in a reasonable and dispassionate manner. The child thereby is led into seeing beyond himself, perhaps not with complete maturity, but with a realization at least of his own inadequacy and with a concept of maturity. This process always involves taking the child where he is, identifying with him, and then proceeding step by step to lead him as far into the process of mature thinking as he can follow. Theoretical? Impractical? Not at all. The best teachers use this device countless times with individual pupils and with the class as a whole to create an awareness of the need for clearer thinking about a particular point of discussion or about a general attitude of the group which may inhibit maximum progress.

QUESTIONS FOR CLASS DISCUSSION

1. What is the general purpose of reading? Are there more specific uses of reading in life?
2. How does the task of the intermediate grade reading teacher vary from that of the primary teacher?

3. What characteristics would you look for in a reading program that allows a child to "create beyond the mere recall of words"?
4. How can teachers determine readiness for content subjects?
5. How can teachers help students differentiate among central ideas, supporting facts and implications?
6. How does reading as a communicative process affect a student's self-concept?

ACTIVITIES FOR FURTHER STUDY

1. Choose an area of interest and make a recreational book list which would guide the reader into progressive levels of difficulty.
2. Talk with other teachers regarding creative methods of sharing interesting books in the classroom. Make a card file for your classroom, showing a variety of ways that students may share books with one another. The students may contribute to the suggestions.
3. As an activity to develop the ability to differentiate between fact and opinion, have two groups debate an issue such as "Who are better drivers — women or men?" A third group in the classroom might set up rules of courtesy to be followed when controversial issues are debated.

SELECTED READINGS

ARTLEY, A. STERL. "Critical Reading in the Content Areas," *Elementary English*, XXXXI (February, 1959), 122-130.

AUSTIN, MARY C. *The Torch Lighters*. Cambridge: Howard University Graduate School of Education, 1961.

BURROWS, ALVINA T. *Teaching Children in the Intermediate Grades*. Boston: D. C. Heath and Company, 1952.

CONANT, JAMES B. *Learning to Read: A Report of a Conference of Reading Experts*. Princeton, N. J.: Educational Testing Service, July, 1962.

DAWSON, MILDRED A., AND BAMMAN, HARRY A. *Fundamentals of Basic Reading Instruction*. New York: Longmans, Green and Co., Inc., 1959.

GANS, ROMA. *Common Sense in Teaching Reading*. Indianapolis: The Bobbs-Merrill Company, Inc., 1963.

HEILMAN, ARTHUR W. *Principles and Practices of Teaching Reading*. Columbus, Ohio: Charles E. Merrill Books, Inc., 1961.

International Reading Conference Proceedings. *Challenge and Experiment in Reading.* Vol. VII. New York: Scholastic Magazines, 1962.

KOTTMEYER, WILLIAM. "Direct Versus Incidental Teaching of Reading Beyond the Primary Grades," *Reading Teacher,* VIII (April, 1955).

McKEE, PAUL. *The Teaching of Reading.* Boston: Houghton-Mifflin Co., 1948.

ROBINSON, HELEN M. *Materials of Reading.* Supplemental Educational Monographs, No. 86, Chicago: University of Chicago Press, 1958.

STONE, CLARENCE R. *Progress in Primary Reading.* St. Louis: Webster Publishing Co., 1950.

WHIPPLE, GERTRUDE. "Characteristics of a Sound Reading Program," *Reading in the Elementary School,* Forty-eighth Yearbook, Part II, National Society for the Study of Education. Chicago: University of Chicago Press, 1959, pp. 33-53.

WITTY, PAUL, AND RATZ, MARGARET. *A Developmental Reading Program for Grades 6 through 9.* Chicago: Science Research Associates, 1956.

YOAKUM, GERALD A. *Basal Reading Instruction.* New York: McGraw-Hill Book Co., Inc., 1955.

THE TEACHING
OF READING
AT THE
FOURTH GRADE
LEVEL

"Open your books to page 87" or, "Let us look together at page 87." How many dull and ineffective lessons are thus begun! If the second opening appears less didactic than the first, it is certainly no more challenging. This is not to say that a teacher never should preface a learning situation with these imperatives. Her next statement or question may be explosive, irritating, challenging, and the full impact of the lesson may be as memorable or shattering as if the teaching period were begun by such an imperative as, "Now all of you throw your reading books out the window; the window will remain closed."

Teachers have long ceased to teach books. Subjects supplanted books. Children followed subjects, the whole child fittingly being taken into consideration. This is not the last word in the philosophy of modern educational procedures. A new era appears to be dawning: *children* are to be taught *subjects*. Retaining the larger measure of emphasis upon the physical — mental — social — moral development of the child as an aim of education, educators are thinking in terms of equipping the child to master subject matter both as a practical asset to the social structure and as a means to the fourfold development of the individual child. This union should prove to be a happy one, especially for the child. He benefits indirectly from consideration of his psychological make-up and the consequent thoughtful presentation of material which it behooves him to master, and directly from expending the effort which he has been challenged to exert to broaden his interests and deepen his understanding.

Determining and Establishing Readiness

The good teacher keeps a figurative finger on the pulse beat of the class as a whole; she knows that overexertion causes a too rapid pulse and that lethargy leads to the opposite extreme. Her aim is to inspire the occasional rapid pulse of challenge, wonder, and ambition, and then to maintain the steadiness of purposeful endeavor. Never can she allow the monotony of mere tasks repeated beyond their usefulness or insignificant details pursued beyond their meaningfulness to delete the fervor of the purposeful and meaningful learning situation. There are at least five factors influencing individual readiness which should be considered separately for each child. Disregarded they will raise problematic blocks to immediate communication and perhaps permanent edifices obstructing complete fulfillment of potential ends.

Attitude toward school. Adjustment to the schedule and routine activities (both work and play) and to the interaction between himself and other children, between himself and teacher, between himself and parents, parents and the school, and between himself and other school personnel and authorities all enter into the child's attitude toward school. Personalities react differently to each other. Occasionally even the previously well-adjusted personality will conflict with that of another to such an extent that the relationship inhibits maximum performance or provokes antagonistic response. A teacher more than anyone else should be aware of a personality clash and should seek to eliminate it. If necessary, she should transfer a child with frequent personality problems to a teacher who would be inclined to recognize and handle the problems objectively. Another problem which a teacher may overlook is the implications of a playground quarrel. A child at odds with a friend is not completely receptive to the most stimulating teaching. Problems stemming from the attitude of the home toward the school can definitely curb successful classroom participation. These can often be averted by a sincere effort on the part of the teacher to take parents into her confidence to promote the best interests of the child, and by a free exchange of ideas and information between the home and school.

If the child is pliable, as indicated by his ready participation in group and playground events, he can be considered to have a favorable attitude toward school, despite his occasional healthy grumbling about overwork and long assignments and his unconcealed anticipation of week ends, recesses and three o'clock.

Attitude toward the learning situation. To distinguish between the school and learning situation it is necessary to think of the school as physical structure — not without a personality, for institutions always have personalities — and the learning situation as the meaningful activity associated with and culminating in the acquirement of knowledge. This latter may be seen falsely as being contained within the school. Actually, it transcends the school. *The learning situation is life, and a school can no more contain it than it can contain life.* The child who comes into contact with a meaningful learning situation in the school carries it from the school, reflects upon it, builds upon it, and incorporates it into his very being. The learning situation, then, occurs within the school, and can be encouraged to some extent, but it can occur in the home, in the Sunday school, at the zoo, on a vacation trip, or in a multitude of places.

The point to be considered is that the child should associate the learning situation with mental and emotional feelings of anticipation and pleasure. The elements of fascination, wonder, satisfaction, self-realization, achievement — one or more of these present in the child's attitude — insure a favorable reception of information and ideas. The natural inclination of every normal child from infancy is to learn. Curiosity is the most general characteristic commonly possessed by children. A contrary attitude toward learning is acquired as a result of conditioning. This may occur in several ways, but it is almost consistently occasioned by the pressures and unfavorable attitudes inflicted and exhibited by well-meaning but thoughtless or uninformed adults. It may occur early in the school experience when the child is engaging in readiness activities.

Consider the case of Susan K. who loved school, loved her teacher, and enjoyed the games, charts and readiness activities which were preparing her to begin reading. Miss West found Susan somewhat immature to begin reading at the end of the average six-week readiness period. Specifically, she needed to strengthen her visual perception skills in distinguishing between abstract formations and letters. Susan's parents did not wish to see her reading instruction delayed, so they obtained some beginning reading materials and attempted to instruct Susan in the evenings. This fostered many unhappy feelings in Susan and was unwise for several reasons. Susan began to share her parents' distrust of the school which she had enjoyed, and her teacher's prestige was lessened. Although her parents did not intend to make her feel intellectually inferior to the classmates who were learning to read, she did begin to entertain feelings of inadequacy as she realized that her parents were disappointed with her lack of progress. Mr. and Mrs. K., in need of proving their diagnostic and remedial procedures, strived harder, displayed overconcern, occasionally became impatient wtih Susan, and lengthened the evening sessions beyond the attention span of even a very mature six year old. A further disadvantage of the situation was that Susan had to forego the leisure of entertainment, play, or other purposeful activity which might have contributed directly to her reading progress both by incidental instructional procedures and by enabling her to find diversion and relief from the more difficult performances of the classroom. Susan entered the second grade the following term with misgivings and feelings of inadequacy. A very enthusiastic and understanding teacher was able, through specialized individual attention to Susan's problem, to recondition her response to the learning situation.

Undesirable pressure may come as a result of comparison with an older brother or sister who excelled in school work. Competition with a child of greater ability, evidence of a teacher's disappointment or impatience with his progress, parental hesitancy to praise his musical, athletic, or dramatic ability because of his lack of scholastic progress — any or all of these can condition the child to respond to the learning situation with distaste. Recognizing the problem and patiently restoring the child's confidence and curiosity, perhaps by experiences which he cannot see as being related to academic achievement, and then consciously creating situations in the classroom which will encourage a transfer of attitude, method, or knowledge to the learning situation are the procedures which recondition the child's attiture toward learning. Nature has provided curiosity and incentive for learning; to insure that these assets are not destroyed, the teacher must be mindful of her duty to teach through them and to preserve them.

Background of experience. Every experience, whether but a fleeting impression or a powerful lesson presented with impact, influences the thought pattern of the child. Some children are prepared by a background of diverse and numerous experiences to receive information and to understand and evaluate ideas. Others coming from impoverished backgrounds must be given experience, firsthand when possible, through the eyes of their more experienced classmates when necessary, through reading, listening, films, pictures, and such trips and excursions as can be feasibly provided by the school. No child ever should be required to learn or to read meaningless material for which he has no preparation and no appreciation. At the fourth grade level, this becomes increasingly important. The child now begins to study geography. Places he has never seen must be made meaningful to him. Can he envision properly the mountainous terrain of the eastern and western parts of the United States if he has spent his entire life on the plains of Kansas? If he lives in the shadow of the softly worn mountains of the East, can he appreciate the peaks, crags, and canyons of the West? Pictures can be helpful; motion pictures of the scenic variety can be useful. A warm and simple story of a child living in such a setting, presented either in an attractively illustrated book or in a good film, can vivify impressions to a much greater extent. To learn the height of a certain peak with no physical concept of how high it really looks from beneath it looking up or from atop it looking down, however, is sheer, utter folly.

The fourth grade pupil must meet George Washington as an adult — a general, a president. But what fourth grade pupil can appreciate a documented study of the American Revolution or of the origin of the United States of America? Out of a background of the cherry tree legend and other stories of the boyhood of George Washington, however, a concept of the stature of the man can be learned. Similarly, out of the Indian fighting in which he engaged, and in which any fourth grade pupil who has been exposed to movies or television has had some vivid secondhand experience, some impression of George Washington, the military strategist, can be achieved. The statesman generally must await an understanding of political concepts, which is a bit mature for the fourth grade pupil. Even here, however, one can make a beginning, drawing upon the song "America," the salute to the flag, and the vague but sincere feelings of patriotism which have been experienced emotionally through song and poetry, if not with full consideration.

Relating Areas of Learning. Another consideration, almost as important as providing the experiential background to learning, is to relate the separate areas of learning to each other and to the total experience of the child. The Catskills encountered by a pupil in geography therefore are the mountains where Rip Van Winkle, about whom we read in literature, is supposed to have slept, and all this is in upper New York State, where the early settlers were largely Dutch, if historical knowledge has extended so far.

Likewise, all of the skills vital to reading a story are employed in the reading of social studies, science, etc. Furthermore, and most important, as the child develops his reading skills through reading a wide range of subject matter designed for his grade level, he acquires information, a knowledge of facts and many impressions which serve as a background for more advanced learning experiences. These, in succession and in time, will prepare him to think more constructively, to evaluate more wisely and to live more effectively. What an enormous challenge to a child to realize that he will become the sum total of his experiences, that the broader and more numerous these experiences, the greater will be his mental growth and the more certain, decisive and satisfying the measures of action he will choose.

Motivation. No single factor can so effectively rob school of its fascination, the learning situation of its interest, and experience of its challenge as simple boredom. The complete lack of motivation or the overuse of certain motivational devices can effect monotony. The teacher who has taught the fourth grade so long that nothing is new has taught too long. She may be twenty-five, but she is a victim of stagnation and senility which need not exist in the very old. Every facet of experience should be new to the teacher not as knowledge but as it creates freshness of response in each new mind which receives it. The first word a baby speaks is not original; it has been heard many times before. To hear it for the first time from him, however, is an experience of delight and wonder. Each class and each pupil in each class will respond with freshness to the material presented, and whether it is being presented for the third or for the thirtieth time, the teacher should be keenly aware of the newness and potential fascination for the pupil.

The teacher must, then, make motivation a general practice to insure the interest which gives momentum to the learning situation. There are specific situations which should always receive special consideration and careful planning in the detail of motivation.

a. Motivational procedures should precede the teaching of a new selection. These should be extended to apply to a new subject, a new chapter, a new unit, a new story. As suggested, the many new fields of subject matter presented at the fourth grade level will require pupil preparation. Together with the task of providing experience in each field and laying the foundation upon which to accumulate knowledge, lies the equal task of giving the child a sense of need in the particular area and a vital interest in delving more deeply into the subject. If the interest is pure — the outgrowth of the desire for knowledge for the sake of knowing or the satisfaction of original or stimulated curiosity — excellent! If the interest is synthetic — the desire for knowledge as a means to some acknowledged end — good! But interest there must be! And at any cost!

b. Motivation procedures should precede the assignment of daily tasks — the activities for group or individual performance. A contest for speed or accuracy, competition between groups, materials or suggestions of play interest, colorful or interesting props are synthetic methods of stimulating increased performance. The pure means of stimulating work for the pleasure and value of working, work for the sheer joy of achieving, and learning because it is a valued end in itself may be limited to the scholarly, but it should not be overlooked. The desire for knowledge or self-improvement runs rather strongly in some children, and their true sense of values should not be reduced to games nor concealed by clever costuming. Motivation, too, must be geared to the needs of the individual. The scholars are to be challenged; the mediocre are to be stimulated; the plodders are to be encouraged to maximum effort.

Readiness factors having been considered, the teacher can turn her attention to the processes and mechanics of the reading situation, realizing, of course, that preparational activities are never concluded as long as there are materials to present and tasks to assign.

Reading as a Mental Process

The primary reading skills have been mastered, and the child at this level has learned to read material with comprehension. He is reading a great deal, if he is reading only what is assigned. The chances are that he is also reading additional material of his own selection because he enjoys reading. Out of his broadening reading experience, he is gaining increased and diversified knowledge, and because he has been taught to read with comprehension, he is retaining information and considering his later reading content in the light of previously or simultaneously acquired knowledge. He is therefore reading critically — not with conscious design, but with equal effect. He may reject a statement or an idea which appears to conflict with earlier information, or he may discard the idea formerly entertained as a result of what he believes to be more valid or later evidence. More often he will simply be building upon previous knowledge and ideas, substantiating and supplementing what he can.

Thought Processes in Reading. Let us examine minutely the thought processes of the child who has just read the story "Brother Francis."[1] Tommy L. was not familiar with the story nor with the life of St. Francis of Assisi. Class presentation for this story included the teacher's telling the story of Androcles and the lion, followed by a discussion of the intelligence of animals and methods of taming and training them. There was also a brief discussion of the setting of the story. Italy was located on a map of Europe, and reference was made to Rome specifically when someone remarked that he had heard the saying, "All roads lead to Rome." Two pupils contributed information regarding Rome which revealed that they held certain vague conceptions of Rome as the seat of early Church history, as the home of the Pope, and as an empire of past grandeur. Hoping not to overshadow the simple beauty of the story by too

---

[1]Ullin W. Leavell, Mary L. Friebele, and Tracie Cushman, *Golden Rule Series, Paths to Follow.* New York: American Book Company, 1956, pp. 176-182.

much explanation from too far afield, the teacher had requested that other comments about the setting be reserved until after everyone had read the story.

Tommy L. thought in this manner as he completed the story. "Brother Francis lived long ago like George Washington, only longer. I wonder if it is a true story. . . I can ask Miss Bartlett when we talk about it together. . . It could be just a story like when George Washington cut down the cherry tree and he didn't really do it — Parson Weem's story, I think it was. . . It would have been possible for George to have cut down the tree. . . Was it possible for a man to talk to a wolf and make him know what he was saying? . . . I think my dog Blacky knows what I say when I talk to him. Sometimes I know he does. . . and sometimes I think I know what he is saying to me. . . I read a book last week that said that dogs and wolves belong to the same family."

Analyzing the mental process outlined, we observe that Tommy was viewing the story critically in terms of its being true. Comparing it with the cherry tree legend, he re-evaluated his thinking in this regard to observe logically that the story could have happened. (Although it did not happen, it was not beyond the realm of possibility.) The possibility of a wolf's understanding a person does not seem so likely. But, he reasons, dogs can understand people. Then, recalling that on the basis of previous reading he knows dogs and wolves to be of the same family, he supposedly concludes that an attribute of a dog might also extend to a wolf. Remarkable? No. Logically sound? Not entirely. It can be imagined, however, that when Tommy has read a thousand more books and used his mind in this manner following each reading, he will have weighed enough facts and made enough conjectures to be thinking soundly and logically and with a predictable degree of accuracy.

Strides are made in reasoning and discriminative thinking as the practice of relating facts to situations, facts to facts, ideas to facts and vice versa, and ideas to situations is developed and encouraged. The teacher can do a great deal to encourage this habit by asking upon every possible occasion, in an incidental manner, questions which relate items of past discussion and reading to the matter under consideration. Previous experience outside the realm of classroom activity should likewise be related to specific learning situations. The question, "Has anyone ever. . .?" usually reveals that one or more members of the class can share an experience with the group. The mind at the fourth grade level has not had enough reasoning experience to be completely logical. Logical thinking can be encouraged, however, as the teacher guides the group thinking process. Just as the third grade teacher sometimes asks questions that put the words in the child's mouth, so the fourth grade teacher asks questions which put the thoughts in the child's mind. The group usually can reason better than the individual, and with the teacher steering the thoughts upon a straight course logical patterns can be facilitated.

Another and final point in this regard is that the more frequently opportunities for relating material, facts, and ideas are provided, the more rapidly a child progresses in the processes of discrimination and logical reasoning. More reading at the proper level enlightens rather than confuses, and more relative thinking develops rather than tires. Any teacher who leads pupils into a more than fragmentary use of the marvelous brain structures at their disposal has made a contribution to humanity, and her influence may be felt in matters of universal consequence.

Reading as a Communicative Process

<u>Silent reading</u>. The development of critical attitudes and opinions as a result of a broader background of acquired information begins, despite its desirability and usefulness in other respects, to close the mind in some instances to further or deeper consideration of certain subjects and to that extent bars communication. Thinking at this stage may result in preconceived

opinions which prejudice the attitude even toward truth, and which inhibit consideration of alien material. Not everyone is aware that Alexander Pope injected the admonition, "Drink deeply," following his often-quoted line,

"A little learning is a dangerous thing."

The fourth grade mind must be taught to drink deeply. One way to accomplish this is to prove occasionally in a planned situation and objective manner that one million people *can* be wrong. The story of Christopher Columbus and his hearty insistence that the world was round, in the face of ridicule and disbelief, is a classic example. The teacher should cite it occasionally, and moralize upon it, or Edgar Guest's "Somebody Said It Couldn't Be Done." She might ask pupils what major changes they have undergone in thinking regarding specific situations since they were four or since they were in the first year of school. Or she may give them the Davy Crockett maxim, "Be sure you're right, then go ahead," with emphasis upon the first imperative. In keeping before them the desirability of weighing the evidence and listening carefully when they cannot listen sympathetically to the other side, the teacher can help to rejuvenate the quality of openmindedness and to encourage its application to the reading situation, enabling unhampered communication.

Once openmindedness is achieved, the situation reverses itself and the pupil must be taught to examine the information his mind has absorbed in the light of past experience, reading and observation. This process may take the form of simple *observation*, as in the case of relating the setting of a story to a geographical location or to the scene of a historical event. It may be a matter of *substantiation* or *corroboration*, as when a statement or event is accepted because it is either in agreement or is interpreted differently but is not in direct conflict with a previously established fact. *Comparing* and *contrasting* are frequently the methods of relating new or different information or ideas to previously acquired knowledge. *Refutation, acceptance,* or *doubt* may result from these processes, accuracy of choice depending upon the limits of experience as well as upon the pupil's ability to see the situation in relation to total experience.

Paradoxically, despite the child's limited experience and his tendency to indulge and defend preconceived ideas, he has an uncanny ability to detect any intentional deception or scheme aimed at presenting a false impression. One young teacher, admitting that her pupils were sometimes better informed in certain areas than she, confesesd that whenever she was asked even the simplest question by a pupil she made a practice of referring it to the group for an answer, thus assuring to herself the prestige of an appearance of knowing what she did not know. The practice of letting the group have an opportunity to answer questions posed by individual pupils is a good one, but even a young teacher may be aware that honesty and humility carry greater prestige than the encyclopedic mind. The humility of the comparatively accomplished teacher at the vastness of both attainable and unattainable knowledge and an honest desire to know more about many things are indeed exemplary to pupils at any level, who, because of the rapidity of their gains, may be lulled into a sense of false accomplishment. The child's ability to "see through" pretentious claims and affectations can be used to advantage as it is directed to the processes of getting total meaning, main ideas, inferences, and important details. Directing its impulsive characteristic by logical reasoning, making full use of the foregoing criteria, i.e., observing, substantiating, corroborating, comparing, contrasting, and accepting, refuting or doubting on these bases, facilitates full communicative impact in reading comprehensively for both stated and implied facts.

Goals of Reading. These processes must be kept before pupils as the conscious goals of reading. Left to chance they would await the results of trial and error which maximum teaching effectiveness can in part eliminate. Pupils must be directed to read for a purpose. Because of her familiarity with the specific content in question and her knowledge of the background of information and experience and the probable degree of insight the pupil brings to the material, the teacher can motivate and insure intelligent reading. Frequently, perhaps daily, the teacher should ask pupils to read for the purpose of improving specific communicative skills. *Getting the total meaning* or *the main idea* logically would be the point of emphasis in reading a selection in which a central theme or idea is expressed. *Getting the implied meaning* by "reading between the lines" is always a challenge, and should be suggested whenever its use might reveal hidden implication, satire, double entendre or other subtlety of indirect expression. Specific questions serve as aids to discovering the subtlety or inference.

A tongue-in-cheek piece of writing might be more aptly discerned as a result of the question: Do you think the author really likes ....? The general question, on the other hand, such as, "What do you think the writer is trying to say?" is too vague and not sufficiently suggestive. Recognition of and appreciation for satire and inference involve a higher form of intelligence and the cultivation of literary taste. The average pupil can be led to see more than the obvious and can come to enjoy the process. *Reading for detailed information* (specified facts, steps in a process, etc.) is frequently the immediate goal in reading a selection from historical, geographical or scientific writing.

It cannot be stated too strongly that pupils should be given these goals in specific terms, preferably in written form on the blackboard for referral is necessary during the reading process. Intelligent reading presupposes a knowledge of purpose. Fourth grade pupils would need discriminatory powers beyond their attainment and clairvoyant powers beyond their potentiality to determine either what the most important facts in a selection in a history textbook are or just which of them the teacher will wish to emphasize.

Oral Reading (as a communicative process). The pupil reading at this level has necessarily read more material silently than orally during the past year. His reading rate may be 200 words per minute, sufficiently in excess of his speaking rate to indicate that he is not vocalizing to any great extent when he reads silently. At this point, many educators feel, and with some justification, that too much attention to the finer points of oral reading will cause vocalization in silent reading and thereby decrease the reading rate considerably. Actually, this situation appears to result only when the attention to oral reading is not distinguished from the reading process, and when there is not a similar emphasis upon silent reading skills and improving the reading rate.

In the author's experience there have been instances of vocalization which retarded the silent reading process, but in each case the causal factor was not the overemphasis of oral reading but the underemphasis of silent reading skills or an inadequate diagnostic and remedial program. A good swimmer out of practice will sacrifice skill and speed, but will not impede his progress by excessive wading if at the same time he devotes an equal amount of time to swimming practice. The discerning teacher, assimilating the previous statements relative to the reading process and the goals of reading, will accept the fact that oral reading alone *is not reading*. Few of the purposes of reading are accomplished in properly assigned oral reading, and in well-prepared oral reading the dramatic and exciting element of sound far outweighs the usual quest for knowledge, as the reader attempts by oral communication to interpret the author's words.

The first grade is not too soon to impress the pupil with the true (although, for him, future) purpose of oral reading: *to inform and/or entertain others*. After the second grade, and to a great extent after the first grade, silent reading skills should be taught, emphasized, and developed. Weaknesses and difficulties should be diagnosed by testing and observing, and corrective and remedial procedures should be instituted the moment the need is indicated. The (silent) reading rate should be increased by a great deal of reading at the proper level, by lengthening the eye-voice span as a part of the visual training program, and by accustoming the pupil to accommodate visual and mental processes in avoiding regressions. Now assuming, as previously, that this program is receiving constant attention and emphasis, increased attention to oral reading is in order. The child whose oral reading habits are neglected finds himself unable to communicate effectively when reading orally; this is true despite the fact that he may be a superior silent reader. Paradoxically, the superior oral reader is almost without exception the superior silent reader. Some of the attributes of good silent reading — comprehension of ideas, facts, moods and tempo — are passed along unconsciously to oral reading, and if enhanced by mechanical and dramatic oral reading skills, make it effective and entertaining.

There are three reasons for increasing attention to oral reading at the fourth grade level. In the first place, the pupil is already an efficient silent reader and has learned to read silently as a process separate from oral reading. Silent reading skills receive even greater attention in the fourth grade as different subject matter is added to the reading program. Second, pupils at this age tend to become self-conscious and to discard the uninhibited speech and behavior characteristics of the primary level. It becomes increasingly important, therefore, to maintain the habit of performing before others, and oral reading is a comparatively innocuous assignment, less demanding than speech-making or debating, less taxing than reciting, and independent of the staging and props required by dramatics. It can be added also that the healthy oral reading situation in the classroom makes for a feeling of unity within the group, which enjoys having a pupil share through oral reading an appealing story, a good joke, or a lovely poem. The learning situation is benefited, and sometimes the good laugh together or the serious discussion growing out of an oral reading will clear the air of individual antagonism and will extend out even to the playground or to the home.

The third reason (and the most relevant) for increasing attention to oral reading skills is that these are transferable habits which improve both the mental processes and the personality. *Voice control and modulation* are integral factors in the pleasing personality, and oral reading provides an excellent opportunity to call attention to unpleasant *pitch* or *tone*. The obligation to read consciously and thoughtfully exists despite the fact that the material has been rehearsed many times. *Concentration in familiar situations* (when woolgathering might be natural) thus is encouraged. The additional obligation to communicate the material to the audience with conversational tone, dramatic effect and appropriate mood fosters the pleasing attributes of *outgoingness* and *consideration*. A person who reads well aloud has learned to be conscious of his ability to affect others pleasantly or unpleasantly and this consciousness is extended to speaking and to writing. Oral reading necessitates listening and the habit of ATTENTION. Mechanical *difficulties can be corrected* during the oral reading process. Proper pronunciation, careful enunciation, and controlled breathing are encouraged as the need for them presents itself. The child at this age can form new habits with greater ease and less chance of regression than he will a few years hence.

The Oral Reading Program. Having presented the case for continuing emphasis upon oral reading simultaneously with increased attention to speed and skills in silent reading at the fourth grade level, we shall observe how this program can be effected. It should be understood, of course, that pupils will not read aloud daily, perhaps less than weekly, but the *emphasis* will be constant. A pupil will be in the stage of selection, preparation, rehearsal, presentation, critical evaluation, or rereading at all times.

Selection. Oral reading selections may come from books or publications used within or outside the classroom. The teacher may wish to approve each selection or to limit selections to types needing emphasis either by individuals or by the group. It is sometimes helpful if the teacher collects a number of anthologies of poetry and short prose selections and some simple one-act plays at the proper level and reads intermittently from them as an aid in selection and as an example in proper oral reading.

Preparation. The following check list should be used by the pupil in preparing the reading for oral presentation.

1. Can I pronounce each word correctly?
2. Am I absolutely certain of the exact meaning of each word in the selection?
3. Does the entire selection have meaning?
4. Do I like the selection so much that I want to share it with others?
5. Have I read the selection silently at least three times?

When all of these questions can be answered affirmatively the pupil is ready for a further stage of preparation, which is so important it warrants separate consideration.

Rehearsal. A good oral reading must be preceded by many practice oral readings. Otherwise, the reading may be intelligent and intelligible, but it might not be properly conversational and communicative. Pupils may be asked to rehearse outside of the classroom on many occasions, but opportunities to learn how to rehearse effectively must be provided first within the classroom, and criteria for proper rehearsal must be presented. This can be handled best in small groups reading parts (in plays) or paragraphs or verses in simple prose and poetry selections. The teacher working informally with these small groups can pinpoint individual weaknesses in communication (failure to look at audience, lack of conversational tone, poor expression, mechanical defects of voice, speech, pronunciation, etc.).

She can prescribe simple methods to be employed in correcting difficulties. "Tell this part to Sue. Now, tell this part to John," etc. . . "Read this sentence. . . Now, close your book and tell me what it said. . . Now, read it again with the same tone you just used in speaking to me. . . Much better. . . See the difference?". . . "How would *you* say that?". . . "Here's a mirror. Read this paragraph to yourself in the mirror. Be sure to look at *you* at least four times, but don't lose your place in the book." . . ."Do you think the people in the back of the room can hear you? Stand in the back and let me read to you. Hold up your hand when you cannot hear me. . . Now, you try reading to me from there." . . ."Pretend your voice is coming up from your stomach. Take a deep breath and talk up and out." (Teacher gives exaggerated demonstration.)

When outside rehearsal is assigned the teacher should have each child present the following list to his listener(s).

1. Does .... (child's name) read in a voice which can be heard?
2. Does .... say all of his words clearly?
3. Does .... read as if he were talking?
4. Does .... look up from the book now and then?

Finer points would be checked by the teacher, but the child who satisfies the listener on the four points listed usually will present a good oral reading. Parents, brothers and sisters, and other pupils ordinarily are good reading critics. Although they may not be the best of readers themselves, they can spot weaknesses as a result of the questions outlined and often can offer the reader constructive tips for improvement.

Presentation. The reading should be presented to a quiet, attentive group prepared to enjoy the performance or to present suggestions for its improvement.

Critical Evaluation. Teacher and pupils should comment upon the reading performance either in appreciation or with suggestions for increasing its effectiveness. It will be necessary at times to make the class presentation a rehearsal period and, following the constructive criticism, to permit the child to polish his reading for later presentation of rereading. Audience reaction is important to the reader and as a criterion for evaluating the effectiveness of the reading. Always give the reader the benefit of displaying his best effort to a number of quiet listeners.

Such an oral reading program is not too time-consuming to be practical. It can be accomplished in fifteen to thirty minutes each day, and each pupil in an average class can read at least once during the week. A teacher who observes this procedure will be fostering unity and entertainment in the classroom, developing the personalities and thinking processes of her pupils, and promoting freedom of expression. Some day she may be pleasantly surprised to witness a return to the now old-fashioned polished political oratory — more pleasing to the ear, if not more loyal to the truth. Her reward will be great if she can reinstitute the unsurpassed custom of families reading aloud together without static, pauses for advertising, poor reception and canned laughter.

Reading as a Pleasurable Process

The general emphasis at the fourth grade level is the broadening and extension of interests and understandings, and the pleasure reading content can and should be used to advantage to expedite the emphasis. At the outset this will be accomplished through material selected by the teacher for reading to the class. Eventually a subtle shift in pupil selections for individual reading will be observable as different tastes are cultivated. With emphasis upon places they have never been, pasts they have not witnessed, and facts they are not prepared to prove there is a danger that pupils will gain an abundance of superficial knowledge unrelated to its component parts, to individual experience, or to total personality. Much can be done to avert this situation by providing interesting, meaningful stories in which vicarious participation or association with previous experience or knowledge is possible. Stories from around the world featuring the experiences of boys and girls in other lands should be used frequently. Stories of boys and girls with a historical setting are helpful. To provide cultural background and depth of understanding the traditional tales and legendary events of other lands and times should be presented. Discussions involving similarities and differences in these events can be helpful.

The spark of poetry should be kept alive at this level also. The fourth grade pupil can become wonderfully intoxicated with words and delightfully enchanted by the words of poetry. James Whitcomb Riley's "Little Orphant Annie," if presented a few weeks before Halloween, will be memorized by some pupils for the occasion. It should be remembered also that Riley wrote "The Man in the Moon" and "The Raggedy Man" to delight children at this age. Eugene Field's fabulously verbose account of "The Dinkey Bird" will actually send them scurrying for their dictionaries, and many lines will be memorized even in the presence of a strong will to resist. Robert Browning's "The Pied Piper of Hamelin" is abundant with the technical charms of poetry and in addition tells a story which will hold any fourth grader's attention intact for the entire reading. The teacher who reads well can read more difficult selections than these and give them meaningful interpretation at the fourth grade level.

From these definite, planned presentations by the teacher there should follow an increased interest in different subjects, in different types of reading material and in an expanded program of individual reading. The rule should be to let the pupils go as far as they will on their own, to provide incentive where it is needed, and to keep the books circulating.

Reading as a Process Requiring the Development of Many Skills

One very essential new skill growing out of the need to read many types of material for different purposes is the *adjustment of rate and reading technique* to the material and reading purpose. This is beneficial each day as the pupil is given definite purposes in the form of questions or instructions to guide his reading. A pupil thus is taught to read at times with care and complete comprehension, at times to get a general idea of the scope of the content, at still other times to get specific infor-

Reading is a Process Requiring Many Skills

mation. Sometimes he reviews material which has been read in one of these ways previously. It is more essential that he know the reading method by which he can, with the greatest efficiency and conservation, gain the desired end in reading than that he achieve that end. He must therefore have considerable practice in *locating information quickly.*

Using the dictionary to get meanings, proper spelling and pronunciation may serve as a beginning point. Quick alphabetizing and finding specific material in alphabetical arrangement should be emphasized. Using the table of contents, index, glossary, maps, charts and graphs is given specific attention until they can be used intelligently and purposefully. *Skimming* for specific information, (observing chapter headings, paragraph headings, key words, etc.) is a valuable skill which should receive attention until it becomes habitual. *Rapid reading* should receive frequent emphasis both as a method of assimilating information and of rereading material which has been studied carefully. Pupils first begin to "study" at the fourth grade level and many need to be taught to study. *Study-type reading* is not merely locating and assimilating information. It may or may not be critical reading. It is purposeful, objective reading interspersed with thinking, noting, summarizing, consulting references, if necessary, and identifying and organizing relevant information. Reading rate usually is not mentioned in connection with studying but the reading, of course, should not be allowed to lag so that the child develops lazy study habits. So long as he is attacking the material with energy and interest and engaging in purposeful activity with proper results he should not be urged to read rapidly.

The words *application* and *examination* appear in the dictionary definition of studying. Perhaps sometimes the word *meditation* might be added to advantage. Considering material in relation to one's total being, examining it and appraising it with one's knowledge and experience, and committing it to future reappraisal on the bases of knowledge and experience to be acquired would more adequately reveal the implications of the word.

Study is man's lifelong approach to an understanding of all that his senses and sensibilities make known to him, and through this understanding comes whatever wisdom or self-knowledge he may attain. Study therefore should never be monotonous or of questionable value. Its methods cannot be explained by a teacher to her class in a comprehensive lecture. They have rather to be made habitual through guided use. The teacher therefore determines in each study situation what emphasis to apply and what method or methods can most economically and successfully promote the achievement of the desired ends. She then gives the pupil definite instructions, preferably in writing, which will insure intelligent and profitable study. It should be added that pupils in the fourth grade cannot be taught how to study. It is a continuing and evolving process. The continuing aspect must be met by each successive teacher even through higher education. The evolving aspect is met by the pupil as his judgment of relevance is increased through directed study, both experimental and experiential, throughout his entire formal education.

The Dictionary. Correlated with the emphasis upon adjusting the reading rate to the type of material and purpose of reading is the presentation of the basic references and sources of information and clarification which are indispensable aids to intelligent study. The initial dictionary skills must be taught at this level. A brief period of drill — five minutes or less, perhaps — and incidental consultation whenever it is useful throughout the day will insure rapid and intelligent dictionary usage as well as an appreciation for the value of the reference source.

Emphasis should be placed first upon *finding a vocabulary entry quickly* by the use of alphabetizing and guide words and by knowing in which fourth of the dictionary the various letters of the alphabet can be found. *Defining a word by discriminating among definitions and contextual uses* should receive fairly frequent formal emphasis and a great deal of incidental emphasis as words are encountered in reading and discussing material. *Determining the correct pronunciation* by using consonant sounds, diacritical marks and accents should receive attention, and the initial strides in determining the pronunciation of a new word independently should be yielding better than chance results. To bring about perfection in this area would require so much concentrated effort and drill at a single grade level that other skills would be neglected or sheer monotony would defeat accomplishment.

Some of the diacritical marks represent such slight and subtle deviations in pronunciation that their use is not completely definable at the fourth grade level or discernible by the fourth grade aural discrimination. Certainly the macron (ā) over a vowel should be readily meaningful as should also the breve (e), since the long and short sounds of the vowels have been clearly defined from the second grade level. Other diacritical marks can be deciphered as the need arises by comparing the mark in question with a known sound so marked in a key word.

Structural Analysis. A great deal of additional review experience and some new concepts in structural analysis techniques should be provided. New prefixes and suffixes should always be noted and defined as they occur. Syllabication should receive review emphasis, and the simpler observations concerning accented syllables should be presented and frequently exemplified. The common occurrence of the accented first syllable in two or three syllable words should be noted. (Examples: soft'ly, won'derful.) Homographic changes resulting from the placement of accents will be both meaningful and interesting. (Examples: con'tract, contract', rec'ord, record'.)

Reading as a Means of Cultivating Oral and Written Self-Expression

Pupils at this level receive their first formal instruction in semantics and usage. During the primary years they received incidental instruction, criticism and correction in these areas. Now they are prepared to examine language structure and from specific examples of accepted usage to make observations and formulate rules which apply generally or with few exceptions. A knowledge of nouns, pronouns, verbs, adjectives and adverbs and their accepted positions in sentence structure equips the pupil to speak more fluently because of increased self-assurance. Selecting synonyms, antonyms and homonyms aids in word choice and increases the vocabulary. Attention to irregular verbs and the pronoun cases gives the child a better grasp of the more difficult areas of selection in which even habitually correct choices cannot always substitute satisfactorily for a knowledge of form. The rare child who always says "It is he" may, when given a choice, question his habit, or be dissuaded from it by incorrect usage on the part of his classmates. If he has been led to see that that the nominative case in pronouns follows all parts of the verb "to be," he can defend his habit and confidently correct his classmates.

Consciousness of correct usage can be fostered by having pupils note errors heard in the classroom or on the playground, including teachers' errors, and permitting them a few minutes each week to divulge the contents of their little black books. This procedure can be effective if errors are corrected and the reason or rule for correct usage in each case is cited and explained. Otherwise, the pupil will benefit his ego more than his language facility; the cat who swallowed the canary would not have had occasion for vanity if he had taken the canary for a mouse.

Correction and Errors. Even the confident, creative child who speaks fluently and writes well needs to follow form in his conversational and literary style. This can be done best *by correcting errors as they occur* and by making certain that each child understands why his choice was incorrect and how to go about correcting it. The writer was closely acquainted with an adult who frequently misused pronouns in compound predicates. (This habit can certainly place a stigma upon a speaker's prestige even among those who are not considerably erudite and who would consciously or unconsciously overlook an error in the use of *who* for *whom*.) Having an occasion to see the notebooks collected and preserved by this adult throughout his educational experience from kindergarten through two college degrees, the writer could not resist the temptation to inspect closely the book marked "Language — Grade Four." Numerous entries of pronoun misusage were apparent, and all of them had gone unnoticed or without correction. Even so, it would be unfair to insist that the school had taught this person to misuse pronouns. He doubtless had acquired the habit through exposure to incorrect usage at home, but an alert fourth grade teacher could have corrected the error each time it occurred, and if it then persisted, she could have devoted individual attention sufficient to correct it.

Ideas do not flee in the face of form; they are more practical sometimes and more communicable always for having been subjected to the rigors of correct and lucid statement. Correct form can be mastered by a fourth grade pupil of average or somewhat below average intelligence, and once it is mastered, it can be made habitual. College instructors of English should not be obliged to teach the rudiments of composition and sentence structure, and pupils who do not continue their education beyond the secondary level should not be guilty of the gross errors in speaking and writing committed to their detriment in job applications and vocational contacts. Needless to say, this is a task which cannot be accomplished within the time limit of one school term at the fourth grade level. The most energetic and comprehensive beginning which can be made at this level should provide a sturdy foundation for the subsequent building of language skills.

The continuing program of extensive pleasure reading is an asset to the cultivation of fluent expression. The auditory impact of rehearsed oral reading increases the ability to discriminate. How often all of us reject an expression not because there is something wrong with it but because it does not "sound right." The ear is trained to good speech, we may say, in much the same way that an ear for music may result from the happy combination of talent or potential ability and exposure to music. (This is not to say that the rules of grammar are not important. The accomplished musician plays a composition as it was written, note by note, in the time and tempo indicated.) It follows then that the more one is exposed to the elements of skillful exposition, literary style and artful expression the keener will be his appreciation from the standpoint of criticism, which he can apply to his own conversation and writing. In the background of every great writer is an avid reader, and most writers find it necessary or helpful to intersperse their creative efforts with reading.

At the fourth grade level the time has come to commit some of the more readable literature to memory. The background of Mother Goose rhymes is not adequate, but a favorite from Robert Louis Stevenson or James Whitcomb Riley or Eugene Field can be memorized with pleasure and profit. Just as the same musical composition can be enjoyed increasingly with each hearing, so the same poem can enchant many, many times and reveal more of its meaning as it is reconsidered. In a world in which the senses and mind are continually bombarded with the claims of rival products and the dubious causes vying for attention, it becomes more and more difficult to pause, examine critically, approach with freshness, gain insight, derive appreciation. Time spent considering, reading, criticizing and appreciating good literature is an investment in individuality, philosophical thinking and improved self-expression, as well as present and future entertainment and insurance against the boredom of which the prophets of increased leisure warn us.

QUESTIONS FOR CLASS DISCUSSION

1. What are the five factors influencing individual readiness?
2. How might folk tales be effectively utilized in the social studies program? Can these be used to develop understandings, attitudes and concepts regarding a particular people?

3. How might a teacher correlate purposeful reading and oral reading? What three reasons might be given for increasing oral reading in the fourth grade?
4. How might biographies be used to develop the skill of comparing and contrasting, as well as to provide for individual differences in abilities?
5. How can a teacher create a "sense of wonder" in her students?
6. Discuss reading goals and practical methods a teacher might employ to achieve them.

ACTIVITIES FOR FURTHER STUDY

1. Make a list of trade books which would enrich and supplement your social studies curriculum.
2. Do a detailed, day-by-day study on a particular student who has a reading problem.
3. Make a diagram of your classroom, noting chalkboard space, bulletin boards, windows, doors, etc. Study various room arrangements that would be conducive to various learning experiences. Does the room have a recreational reading center?

SUGGESTED CLASSROOM MATERIALS

Story Collections:

ANDERSEN, HANS CHRISTIAN. *Andersen's Fairy Tales.* Yonkers, N. Y.: World Book Company.

Child Study Association of American (Compilers). *Castles and Dragons.* New York: Thomas Y. Crowell Company.

DEPEW, OLLIE (Compiler). *Children's Literature by Grades and Types.* Boston: Ginn and Company, 1938.

FENNER, PHYLLIS (Editor). *Time to Laugh.* New York: Alfred A. Knopf, Inc., 1942.

JOHNSON, EDNA, AND OTHERS (Compilers). *Anthology of Children's Literature;* second edition. Boston: Houghton Mifflin Company, 1948.

Poetry Collections:

Association for Childhood Education, Literature Committee. *Sung Under the Silver Umbrella.* New York: The Macmillan Company, 1935.

FERRIS, HELEN (Compiler). *Favorite Poems Old and New.* New York: Doubleday & Company, Inc., 1957.

PETERSON, ISABEL J. (Editor). *The First Book of Poetry.* New York: Franklin Watts, Inc., 1954.

Play Collections:

HARK, MILDRED, AND McQUEEN, NOEL. *Special Plays for Special Days.* Boston: Plays, Inc.

STEVENSON, AUGUSTA. *The Red Shoes and Other Plays.* Boston: Houghton Mifflin.

Films and Filmstrips:

Coronet Films, Chicago, Illinois.

Curriculum Films, Inc., Tujunga, California.

Society for Visual Education, Inc., Chicago, Illinois.

Recordings:

American Book Company, New York, New York.

Children's Record Guild, New York, New York.

Columbia Records, Inc., New York, New York.

Folkways Records and Service Corp., New York, New York.

Recreational Reading:

CARLSON, NATALIE SAVAGE. *The Family Under the Bridge.* Pictures by Garth Williams. New York: Harper and Bros., 1958.

MEINDERT, DE JONG. *Wheel on the School.* Illustrated by Maurice Sendak. New York: Harper, 1954.

WHITE, E. B. *Charlotte's Web.* Illustrated by Garth Williams. New York: Harper, 1952.

SELECTED READINGS

ANDERSON, IRVING H., AND DEARBORN, WALTER F. *The Psychology of Teaching Reading.* New York: The Ronald Press Co., 1952.

DARBY, O. N. "The Place of and Methods of Teaching Oral Reading in the Elementary School." *Elementary School Journal,* Ll (March, 1951), 380-88.

ELKINS, ANNICE DAVIS. "The Problem of Reading Geography," *Education,* LXXVII (September, 1956), 37-44.

GRAY, WILLIAM S. *On Their Own in Reading.* Chicago: Scott, Foresman, 1960.

HANNA, GENEVA R., AND MCALLISTER, MARIANNA K. *Books, Young People and Reading Guidance.* New York: Harper and Row, 1960.

HARRISON, M. LUCILLE. *Reading Readiness.* Boston: Houghton Mifflin Co., 1939.

JOHNSON, LOIS V. "The Process of Oral Reporting." *Elementary English,* XXXV (May, 1958), 309-13.

LARRICK, NANCY. *A Teachers Guide to Children's Books.* Columbus, Ohio: Charles E. Merrill Books, Inc., 1960.

LEE, J. MURRAY, et al. "Measuring Reading Readiness." *Elementary School Journal,* XXXIV (May, 1934), 656-66.

MIEL, ALICE, ed. *Individualizing Reading Practice.* New York: Bureau of Publications, Teachers College, Columbia University, 1958.

NORVELL, GEORGE W. *What Boys and Girls Like to Read.* Morristown, N. J.: Silver Burdett Co., 1958.

OGILVIE, MARDEL. *Speech in the Elementary School.* New York: McGraw-Hill Book Company, Inc., 1954.

PRESTON, RALPH C. *Teaching Study Habits and Skills.* New York: Rinehart and Company, Inc., 1959.

ROBINSON, HELEN M. "Factors Which Affect Success in Reading." *Elementary School Journal.* LV (January, 1955), 263-69.

SAPIR, EDWARD. *Language: An Introduction to the Study of Speech.* New York: Harcourt, Brace and World, Inc., 1949.

TRAUZER, WILMER K. *Language Arts in Elementary Schools.* New York: McGraw-Hill Book Company, 1963.

THE TEACHING
OF READING
AT THE
FIFTH GRADE
LEVEL

CHAPTER *3*

What's the good of Mercater's North Poles and Equators,
Tropics, Zones, and Meridian Lines?
So the Bellman would cry: and the crew would reply
They are merely conventional signs!

LEWIS CARROLL

Whether one is snark hunting or teaching the fifth grade,
planning is essential. The signs on the map may be conventional,
but they are so because they are vital. Lest the fifth grade teacher
be tempted to discard too many of the proven methods while an
exhuberant class wafts her along upon its enthusiasm, the foregoing words of caution are injected. Fifth grade pupils character-
istically are enthusiastic. The new vistas opened by the expand-
ing content of the fourth grade curriculum have whetted
appetites for larger servings of the same varieties. Questions have
arisen daily as pupils have glimpsed new horizons. Those which
come up conceivably could carry pupils into a dozen different
fields of discovery from which reunion would be difficult, if not
impossible. Shall the teacher pursue these areas of wonder or not
pursue them? Shall she permit haphazard flights in all directions,
or suppress the desires to learn about specific things and quench
the self-motivating forces which prompt them?

Planning the Program

Fortunately, the teacher finally can provide at the fifth grade
level for both the necessary adherence to the curricular demands

and the flights of fancy which can be informative and also adapted to the perfecting of reading skills, if not to conformity with the curriculum. The emphasis upon the use of reference materials makes possible the twofold teaching feat described, and the oral or written reports or discussions which result can be turned to very constructive and effective instructional devices, as will be seen. An over-all plan is vital, however, to prevent indulgence of the tendency to wander too far afield. Specific plans must be made, adjusted, and made over, to insure that essential items are not neglected. Often the teacher can appear to go along with the whims which must be indulged, but underneath there should be "more method and madness" in the flight. Without method, the snark will be gone, and the map devoid of conventional signs will be of no use in the homeward voyage.

Effective planning will consider the individual needs of pupils and the activities in which the group as a whole can participate. It should be noted that each section of this (and the previous) chapter deals with teaching reading not to a specific grade, but at a specific level. For this reason, the discussion of grouping has been omitted. Grouping is, of course, essential among heterogenously assigned pupils, and despite the instructional advantages of homogeneous grouping, the stimulating effect of associating with superior readers and the habit of considering and helping those who must go slowly offer incentives to progress and to social arts. Generally speaking, however, the material presented here may be applied to teaching reading at the fifth grade level, whether to pupils in the fifth grade classroom in the average group, in the fourth grade classroom to the superior group, or in the sixth grade classroom to the retarded group. Perhaps it should be observed at this point that many individual needs can be met while the group is working together on a project, activity, or topic or interest, if planning and materials are adapted to individual requirements. Pupils can be guided to the materials at their proper levels, preparation and individual study, but general plans, discussions, contributions, reports, projects, and evaluations can and should include everyone.

Independent Reading. Fifth grade readers are sophisticated, tossing around vague statements such as, "I read somewhere one time that . . ." Reading has become a reflex, and so much reading experience has been gained that the entire outlook has been affected by fragmentary or unremembered information and ideas either read or surmised as a result of reading. Here guidance in corroborating or discounting beliefs is essential. An acquaintance with source material, references, the location of materials in the library, and the quickest method of determining the validity of the source, in view of the point in question, is the vital need of a pupil reading at the fifth grade level or beyond. The time has come, too, for intelligent discrimination and effective organization of materials. Much reading will be independent and quite a bit of it will be relatively unguided. For example, the pupil will be reading material for a report on a topic of individual interest or need, and the teacher may not be familiar with either the topic or the material. The pupil therefore will find himself faced with the problem of realizing his aim in reading by selecting pertinent information, note-taking, outlining, classifying, comparing sources, selecting and organizing information, and finally presenting it to the group orally or submitting it in written form in a lucid, pleasing manner or style. Whereas the reading so described must be somewhat unguided, care must be taken that it never be misguided, uncertain of its purpose, or meaningless from the pupil's viewpoint. The skills which make possible this accomplishment comprise most of the fifth grades reading program and are considered here as they apply in the previously listed points of emphasis.

Reading as a Mental Process

Because the pupil reading at this level must utilize the basic reading skills practiced from the directed pre-reading period described in the section on readiness through each successive level to the present, because he must make his reading meaningful by enlightening it with his own experience, and because he must now determine to a large extent what and why he will

read and the significance of what he reads, it will be helpful to analyze the thought processes which will insure intelligent, purposeful reading.

An Ability to Follow the Meaning and Thinking of the Author.
This ability is the first major thought process essential to reading at this level. It is relatively simple to follow an illustrated
lecture on a given subject. Voice inflections, slower procedure,
additional explanation, visual aids and an opportunity for asking questions make the lecture an indispensable aid in deriving
understanding from difficult material. The listener is at all times
the object of the same amount of consideration as is given to
the lecture topic. This is even more applicable to storytelling
or the theater which seek to carry the listener along to the meaning by capturing his emotional machinery, thereby forcing his
concentration so as to insure the maximum mental response
of which he is capable. The author, on the other hand, deprived
of his audible voice, must depend upon the ability of his reader
to substitute skillful reading for voice inflection, emphasis, discussion and clarification of the content.

If all textbooks at the fifth grade level were written with
this factor in mind, the teacher's plight would be considerably
relieved. Many fifth grade textbooks are written more for the
purpose of imparting information regarding their particular subjects than to promote a pleasurable attitude toward study and
to develop reading skills. Such books are not scientific from the
educational viewpoint, regardless of how much scientifically
accurate information they contain. The teacher who is confronted
with the problem of using such textual materials will find it
necessary to rely upon her own resourcefulness and the interests of the group to build units which a more adequately con-
ceived text would have accomplished. The poorly written text
can serve as a reference, and the reading skills of skimming,
locating desired information quickly, classifying and organizing
material, etc., can be expedited. Planning and forethought alone
can make such materials useful, and exercises and activities must
be devised and created by the teacher to insure that pupils will

not develop undesirable attitudes toward history, geography, language and science merely as a result of unpalatable presentation.

Every subject is of consuming interest to a great many people, and every subject can be of at least a passing interest to everyone if it is presented in such a way that it satisfies a personal need or appeals to the pleasurable emotions. It is indeed unfortunate that those who are authorities in certain fields lack the understanding that others may not be at all enamored of their subjects and the enthusiasm that might enable them to present them attractively to others. Nevertheless, the teacher must not excuse herself from the task of compensating for poorly written material, and she must, deplorable as it is, take care not to diagnose reading as poor when the inability to follow the meaning and thought is really a result of poor writing.

The ability to follow the meaning and thinking of the author requires at least four classes of skill development. First, the pupil must have a *command of the mechanics of reading* (word recognition skills, knowledge of sentence structure and punctuation, adequate eye-voice span). Second, he must have the *ability to concentrate his attention upon the material at hand* so that he can comprehend the meaning of the words he reads and gain an abstract understanding of their interaction in conveying information and ideas. Third, *he must be able to weigh the facts and ideas critically* to determine the relative significance of the various aspects presented and the over-all purpose of the content. Fourth, and perhaps last, *he must be able to accomplish the aforementioned tasks with a speed appropriate to the level and type of material and the purpose in reading.*

An adequate program of testing accompanied by careful observation of actual performance for each individual will reveal in which avenue there is weakness. The foregoing four headings should serve as a guide in diagnosing the type of difficulty, and the items which come under each heading should serve as a check list to pinpoint the definite weaknesses. When

To Follow the Author's Meaning Requires Many Abilities

the weaknesses are discovered, remedial procedures should be instituted at once and continued until testing and performance demonstrate that they are no longer needed. Many exercises and activities relating to each type of skill perfection can be selected from the numerous workbooks and published materials which every teacher should have available for supplementing instruction. Teachers frequently can, and sometimes prefer to, prepare a large portion of their own exercises for remedial purposes so that they tie in closely with the class activities in which the pupil is engaged. Needless to say, despite the additional time required in adequate planning and composing of exercises, the teacher will receive dividends in interest, spontaneous motivation, and speedy response upon her investment in the time necessary to plan interesting, related exercises.

Relating Thought to Experience. Growing out of, and yet additional to, the ability to follow the meaning and thinking of the author, is the *ability to relate the thought and meaning to total experience,* that is, to previously acquired knowledge, to present situations and simultaneous pursuits, and (whenever possible) to an anticipation of future needs, uses, and interests. Here, too, practice is essential. Past experiences often must be estimated by the teacher, presented to the pupil's attention and revitalized in his thinking for adequate association. Hints and suggestions must be given to facilitate the relation to simultaneous pursuits. Encouragement must be offered to insure that vital bits of information and ideas of consequence are filed mentally for evaluation in terms of future experience.

It should be remembered that mental growth through reading is a guided process. It demands that the teacher have a projected vision of mature thinking and logical reasoning for each of her pupils and that she guide the process intelligently and incidentally as well as formally and instructionally. It demands that the magic wand of motivation be frequently waved to force interest and curiosity and that the inestimably valuable element of enthusiasm be injected into the performance of tasks, the discussion of ideas and the readily enticing wonders of life and business of living and learning.

Reading as a Communicative Process

Silent Reading. All that has been presented under this heading at the previous grade level is still vital and must receive continued emphasis. The previously described communicative situation begins, however, to reverse itself at this level. Whereas formerly the pupil began with reading and then proceeded to the problem, now he frequently begins with a problem which he attempts to solve through reading. He must therefore select his sources of information, receive from them what they communicate specifically in relation to his particular problem or need, compare and contrast the contributions of various sources and the viewpoints of different authors, and then proceed with the assimilation, organization and presentation which will be discussed under separate headings.

Communication, then, becomes selective. The pupil decides not to subject himself to all that an author has to say, but rather to discover what he has to say about one particular item in answer to his problem and needs. Reading, then, becomes a matter of purpose, of pupil-prescribed purposes, which it has not been before. Guidance, now, is fourfold. The pupil must be aided in stating and understanding his problem or need, in determining what sources can provide solution or aid, in locating the essential material quickly and conservatively, and in applying the assimilated information concretely to the matter at hand. Adequate reference materials in the room and frequent access to the library are the material needs which must be met. Planned and incidental, purposeful use of such materials is the means to progress. Constructive use of the information obtained and guidance in its effective compilation and presentation are the ends which give meaning and purpose to the process.

Care must be taken that the selective type of communication involved in the use of references does not obscure or diminish the skills formerly emphasized as vital to the communicative process. Getting the precise meaning, main idea, or details of significance remains extremely important, and these skills continue to be generally emphasized. Daily situations in all types of reading and study provide for and actually demand their emphasis. The danger is that the more literary communicative skills will be neglected as the quest for factual information excludes the imaginative, fictitious, and satirical writings from the daily reading schedule. Pupils infrequently exposed to humor, irony, and satire will neither recognize nor discern them. The mental exercises of anticipating the author, grasping his implications, interpreting critically what he is attempting to say and evaluating the truth and effect of his statements cannot be injected into factual accounts. Provision must be made for including selections of literary worth in the curriculum. Pupils must not spend all of their time leaping from history to geography or from the encyclopedia to the atlas, although the ability to obtain information quickly from these sources is a point of major emphasis.

In line with the cultivation of varied interests, books and stories of literary value have been written dealing with historical heroes and times, geographical settings and scientific guests. In many of them, bits of homespun philosophy, inference, and cause and effect relationships can be found. The teacher should seek out such books and stories and bring them to the attention of the group. These and other types of literary works can be used in the program of pleasure reading, and valuable skills of discernment and appreciation can be cultivated as a result of guided discussion of the literary elements and merits of specific selections.

An example of integrated material is the fifth grade reading textbook, *Frontiers to Explore* by Leavell, Friebole, Cushman.[1] This book makes adequate provision for synchronizing the various factual pursuits of fifth grade pupils and enhancing the

---

[1]*The Golden Rule Series*, American Book Company, 1956.

pursuits with fictitious flavor, vicarious association and literary elements. Three of the six units contained in the book deal with historical and geographical facts. "Young Americans of Yesterday," "Young People of Other Lands" and "Stories of Great Americans" together comprise approximately half of the reading text. All of the stories contained in these three units lend themselves to adaptation in the perfection of communicative skills.

In the story "By Touch Alone," pp. 302-309, the pupil is led to increase and expand his understanding of a problem in communication. The story of Ann Sullivan's acute problems in teaching Helen Keller to communicate by touch can be used to bring about a basic understanding of the importance of and need for communication. Natural curiosity about those who are different causes the pupil to note minutely the detailed handling of the instructional process. Inferences can be made about the characters and personalities as suggested by their actions and behavior. The teacher might call these to the pupil's attention by skillful questioning. What do we learn about Helen from her independent search for the doll? (Helen had "asked" Miss Sullivan for her doll by holding out her arms with a rocking motion. Miss Sullivan, wishing her to learn to shape the letters d-o-l-l with her hands in asking for the doll, ignored Helen's less acceptable means of making her request. Helen stubbornly refused to comply with her teacher's wishes and began her independent and somewhat frantic search for her doll.) Pupils will be led to observe that the independent spirit and determination which prompted Helen to act as she did in this situation made it possible for her to exert the tremendous effort necessary to learn to communicate effectively and, indeed, remarkably. Similar questions about both Helen and Miss Sullivan would invoke inferential thinking, logical deduction and intelligent response. This particular story also aids indirectly in a way not explicitly intended by causing the child to view his own fortunate situation in relation to Helen Keller's condition and to resolve to dedicate his five senses to their fullest accomplishment.

Another story from the same text, "African Adventure," (pp. 120-127) holds the child's attention through the medium of well-written breathtaking adventure while the local color, imagery, literary style and impressions of cultural significance infiltrate the thinking. Sentences such as these lend enchantment to the exciting account of the action:

Ropy vines hung from their branches.
The feather of the arrow swept his cheek.
And the wind of his passing was like the chill of death.
Great danger makes all men brothers.

The rapt attention necessary to follow the action receives these descriptive passages incidentally, so the pupil is given maximum exposure to the literary elements. He will infer that Africans who have not read at all are better equipped to anticipate and outwit their natural enemies than white visitors who have studied and read much about the continent. If guided toward the observation, he will also infer that Africans have a cultural heritage, which, although unlike western tradition, is worthy of respect and can be applied to advantage by any peoples. Vicarious participation in the exciting adventure will impart the total meaning and implications of the action at least subconsciously upon the child's mind. The conscious process of enumerating, stating, and evaluating will, of course, require guidance. The teacher should insist upon the use of textbooks and supplementary materials with meaty, well-written stories. There should always be stories which permit vicarious participation in intriguing situations. They should be written in a literary rather than in a journalistic style, however, and they should give rise to further reflection, to inferential thinking, and to self-examination. The full effect of communication is not achieved when one receives mentally the gist of the statements of the author.

For the impact which characterizes communication the process of abstract thinking must interpret the message against the background of total experience and within the frame of reference drawn from the experience of all that is applicable to the present area of consideration. Then, and only then, is understanding added to mental reception. Without this basis of acceptance, information and ideas are like a drop of blood on a microscopic slide manifesting its component parts but not the total impression of its capabilities as a life-giving substance. Much of man's education is so limited. Knowledge itself is limited to the finite potentialities of the human mental structure, but it is limited even more by the shrinking of the thought structure from engaging in the processes which would assimilate, reflect, examine and compare until the end result would approximate whatever degree of wisdom is potentially attainable.

Oral Reading. Again the prepared oral reading should be given its proper place in the reading program. The tape recorder should be introduced into the classroom at the fifth grade level. Pupils are conscious of deviations in the speech patterns about them and they are aware of unpleasant pitch and tone in their classmates' voices. They have had enough experience with dramatics to be captivated by the glamour of the theater. They are ready to benefit from formal instruction in vocal and dramatic skills. A good beginning point is the act of listening to a recorded dramatization or narrative-drama. Many excellent ones are available and should be a part of the school's record library. A favorite can be played repeatedly until pupils are familiar with the characters and have memorized a number of the lines. Pupils can then be asked to select a line for recording once in the normal speaking voice with the expression natural to the individual and once in imitation of the tone and expression used by the actor or actress. Pupils will be amazed at their lack of expression and will become conscious of speech and voice faults and of the need for expression in speaking and reading.

Some exercises and activities which can be used effectively at this stage (and recorded if time permits) are presented here.

Have pupils read sentences such as the following to give a variety of different interpretations.

I wonder why she did that. (*You* may know.)
I *wonder* why she did that. (I'll probably never *know.*)
I wonder *why* she did that. (She must have had a reason.)
I wonder why *she* did that. (Anyone else I might understand.)
I wonder why she *did* that. (If only she had just *thought* about it.)
I wonder why she did *that.* (Some other action would have been understandable.)
I wonder why she did that? (Not on your life; I *know!*)
I wonder why she did that! (Utterly disgusting!)
I wonder . . (reflective pause) . why she did that. (Perhaps if I put myself in her place, I shall know.)
I wonder why she did . . . (sneering pause) . . . that. (That unspeakable thing!)

The first six interpretations involve a change of emphasis resulting in a change in meaning. Pupils will make a game of repeating sentences in this manner, but this is not the place to stop. The next two interpretations are changes in attitude; the last two require emotional interpretation, the first perhaps expressing pity and the other scorn or hatred, depending upon the exact expression, tone and intensity of speaking. Pupils should learn by attempting to "feel" themselves into a situation or by copying the tone of a good actor or actress to run the gamut of emotions in their speaking. Sadness, exultation, pity, fear, hatred, etc., have been experienced by fifth grade pupils, and to apply emotion to speech and oral reading not only increases the effectiveness of presentation and communicative skills but adds an essential dimension to understanding as an experience of total personality.

Many sentences from the daily reading experience will lend themselves to numerous interpretations. Additional exercise can be provided with such as these:

I was only trying to help.
Perhaps he will change his mind.

I have seen him before.
You are forgetting something.
Things will be different now.
I think we should wait awhile.

Different meanings, attitudes, and emotions can be read into each of these, and reading skills of mental interpretation and dramatic communication are simultaneously improved.

Choral Reading. Exercises in choral reading are particularly effective because they present an opportunity for class preparation and analysis prior to presentation. Another advantage of such selections is that pupils are less self-conscious and inhibited when reading in unison. Two or three silent readings for the purpose of getting the mood, theme or story, and reading instructions should precede the class analysis of the selection by parts. Individual pupils should be permitted to demonstrate what they feel to be the appropriate tone and expression for each part, and the class should criticize these suggestions, accepting, improving, or rejecting them. The teacher should guide this process and if necessary also serve as a model for imitation. Several rehearsals which may be interrupted for suggestion or demonstration should precede the final presentation. Exaggerated expression of each part by the teacher sometimes prepares the class to give correct expression or proper tone where needed. Choral readings must not be limited to those designed for the purpose. Any suitable poems or lovely prose which the class enjoys can be arranged by the group for choral reading.

Dramatization. Dramatizations written by pupils, based upon favorite stories, or selected as such offer an excellent and appealing means of improving expression. Few plays contain enough parts for an entire group, but this problem can be solved either by permitting the simultaneous production of several plays by the different reading groups or by assigning each part to be prepared by several pupils and holding tryouts for the selection of the cast. Whenever interest and staging possibilities are conducive to proper presentation the teacher should encourage the performance for the entertainment of another class or classes. The many opportunities for constructive activity, problem solving and cooperative endeavor afforded by staging a performance far outweigh its inconveniences and time-consuming aspects. Remembered lines, scenes, and emotions linger long after the dates and details of great campaigns are but vague impressions, and the world of fantasy, after all, has a peculiar reality all its own.

The individually selected and prepared oral reading should continue to receive attention. When choral or dramatic activities or group studies in interpretation are taking place these readings may be omitted, but certainly every fifth grade pupil should share an interesting and well-executed reading experience with the group several times each month.

Reading as a Pleasurable Process

It is frequently at about the fifth grade level that tastes become very distinguishable as to sex. The teacher finds it more difficult, therefore, to select worthwhile materials to read to the entire class. The girls would be very much inclined to listen to Louisa Alcott five days each week if the boys could tolerate it. The boys, on the other hand, would find Samuel Clemens fascinating as a steady diet if the girls could survive it. A few girls always find Tom Sawyer and Huck Finn interesting characters, but the Alcott books are almost always regarded by boys at this age as sentimental twaddle. On one point there is agreement: it is desirable to have the teacher read to the class. The hero stories continue to be fairly popular with boys and girls as a better acquaintance with the historical facts of their lives adds prestige to their appeal. Tales of high adventure and suspense never lack an attentive audience, and although these generally are confined to the good rather than great writers, they are, nevertheless, worthwhile.

The legends of ancient cultures and stories based upon them are excellent for story interest, historical background, and as exercises in philosophy. American Indians, specifically, form a fascinating study for boys and girls at the fourth and fifth grade levels, and there is an abundance of good literature on this subject. (Needless to say, a great deal of poor and mediocre writing concerning Indians also exists. In selecting new material spot read a few of the pages here and there for imagery, description, style and beauty of expression.)

Hiawatha, especially his childhood, is meaningful and interesting to the fifth grade pupil. The teacher should precede its reading with the Indian legends which served Longfellow as source material. The legendary Indian Manabozho was a model for Longfellow's *Hiawatha.* The legends, originally collected by Henry Rowe Schoolcraft, an early ethmologist and writer on American Indians, appear in many anthologies and books, some of which can be found in any good school library. Hiawatha is a fresh, living reality when presented with the proper background at the fifth grade level. His questions and discoveries are the subjects of wonder and interest in every child; the child at this age who sits with Hiawatha on the shores of Gitchee Gumee reflects enough of the shining big sea water to welcome the return of his little friend at an age when the remainder of his story will be more meaningful. He will learn, too, that the love of the poet, the wondering of the primitive, and the dreams of mankind have a place of their own in the unfathomable mysteries of life and the universe which remain the riddle of the ages.

Poetry. Fifth grade pupils are ready or can be prepared to read poetry on their own. The comical, the whimsical, the shocking and the narrative types are especially appealing. Even the acknowledged poetry haters will show a burst of uncontrolled appreciation for Thayer's "Casey at the Bat" and for Gilbert's "Yarn of the Nancy Belle". Pupils should listen to poetry read well by the teacher or on records before they are given much of it to read independently for pleasure. Some of it should be memorized either as a conscious process or as a spontaneous result of hearing it repeatedly. Every teacher has her favorites, and it is these which the class will receive from her and demand again and again until the poems become a part of them. Poetry can be extremely pleasurable or unbearably painful, depending upon its presentation. Some of the elements of the pleasurable presentation of poetry are given here.

1. Poetry is enjoyed in terms of experience. Pupils must either have the background or be prepared by receiving the necessary experience for enjoying a particular poem. The teacher must keep in mind when she selects poetry for the group that there is a wide discrepancy between her experience and that of the fifth grade, and that the poetry which is vital and beautiful to her may be an anathema to her class. A few incomprehensible poems will do no harm occasionally. The child may not know what it is to "wander lonely as a cloud," but he has almost certainly been enchanted by the beauty of a profusion of blooming daffodils. Although solitude holds no bliss for him, he will be, in reading the simpler poems of Wordsworth, preparing his "inward eye" for increased reception.

2. Although the reader may be capable of understanding a poem, he may become lost in the maze of form and technicality and miss the meaning. Most of us could not immediately paraphrase the hymns and anthems we have sung for many years. Indeed, we are often startled when we analyze their words for meaning. The tunes are pleasant; the words are known by rote; we go no further. The rhythm of poetry, the prevalence of imagery, and other distracting technical devices can, if approached without a knowledge of design and purpose, be consuming elements in themselves. The reader hypnotized by the flow of words catches an occasional, fleeting suggestion or image and is lost again in alliteration, assonance and meter. He completes his reading with little or no consciousness of the meaning of what he has read. The only way to correct this situation is to remind pupils that with each poetry reading they are to read as if the selection were a story. The teacher can set an

example by always reading poetry intelligently and interpreta-tively, using the punctuation marks for the purpose for which they were intended. This is not to say that attitudes and emo-tions should not be interpreted by expression and tone to an even more pronounced degree than in prose reading. The metri-cal and rhythmic aspects should, however, receive no special treatment, natural reading giving them sufficient emphasis.

3. Anthologies and collections containing poetry suitable and readable at the fifth grade level should be available, and their use should be encouraged, motivated, and if necessary, insured by formal reading or assignment. Only by exposure to poetry do pupils feel at home in the medium.

Reading as a Process Requiring the Development of Many Skills

Organization of Materials. The new group of skills intro-duced at this level relates to the organization of material. *Note-taking* is the most essential of these and the easiest to teach. By providing group practice in selecting important points from a factual account or reference and demonstrating the abbrevi-ated and incomplete technique of rapid note-taking the teacher can bring about an awareness of the practical use of the method. While this skill is being initiated much incidental practice can be provided in study-type reading and reference work. Group selection and evaluation of individual selection of important points in a reading are excellent means of cultivating discrimina-tion between important and insignificant details.

Outlining follows note-taking and should be presented first as a method of handling selections which have only one major point to make and several details regarding this particular point. When pupils show ability to state the major heading and to itemize related details they may proceed to selections which contain two ideas or points with facts related to each, and so on. Outlining is an excellent method of studying reading and of logical analysis of the organization, purpose and scope of material. It should be observed that the organizational skills are new only in the form which they require. Getting the main idea or ideas and relevant points or details in sequence have long received major emphasis.

Summarizing also gains impetus as reference reading, for the purpose of making reports becomes a feature of classroom activity. Note-taking or outlining is valuable preparation for the oral or written summary. This fact is easily proved to pupils by having them read a selection and attempt to summarize it without notes or outline, and then by having them reread the selection, making notes or an outline from which to give the summary. Both the ease and the completeness with which the project can be executed will assert the value of the organizational procedures.

Versatility. As can be anticipated, with the emphasis upon reference materials and organization, *versatility* is a continuing element of importance in the reading process. To know immediately just what degree of comprehension is required by the content in question, to be fully aware of the reading purpose, and to be able to adjust the rate and technique to the content are vital skills in discrimination. Much guided practice will establish the different reading techniques as skills. The entire class may follow a "skimming" process by the teacher. Then, a purpose (or some points to find) in skimming another selection independently may be offered. Pupils will progress at different rates. Some will be able to coordinate the visual and mental processes so that the eyes will move quickly to the desired information while the brain records it and rejects what is not worthwhile or the point in question. Others will find it difficult for some time to register mentally the selections made as a result of the co-ordinated performance of eyes and mind.

In addition to the numerous exercises in any good worktext or supplementary workbook which provide practice in the various types of reading there is endless opportunity throughout the day, regardless of whether the subject is history, geography, science, language, arithmetic or reading, to provide directed practice in adapting rate and method to the content and purpose. The teaching of reading skills can not be compartmentalized into one period. It must be a conscious and an incidental process in every area of reading, and it must have a formal ending only when formal education is completed. Whether the purpose can best be achieved by rapid reading, skimming, or study-type reading should be determined. The teacher can at first explain which type is best in view of the stated purpose. Later the group can decide together which type to employ, and when this method reveals general discretion, the individual can be left free to choose his own method.

Word Recognition. The *word recognition skills* continue to receive emphasis at this level. The phonetic skills are re-emphasized through dictionary usage. Structural analysis skills, including syllabication, prefixes, suffixes, root words, plurals, possessive forms, contractions, compound words, etc., receive continued emphasis and are presented in increasingly difficult exercises. Rules are presented as inductive processes and are applied deductively in specific situations.

The Dictionary. Pupils receive a great deal of experience in employing the dictionary and should become familiar with diacritical marks and all possible dictionary uses. The following check list of dictionary skills is followed by a check list of diacritical marks. (These marks are no longer emphasized as they were a few years ago, but are, nevertheless, included here for the teacher's benefit.)

1. Location of words
   a. Using alphabetical order.
   b. Using guide words.
   c. Knowing in what approximate portion of the dictionary each letter is found.
2. Defining words
   a. Choosing definitions to suit context.
   b. Choosing synonyms.
   c. Identifying root word.

3. Pronouncing words
   a. Knowing consonant sounds.
   b. Noting silent (omitted) consonants.
   c. Using respellings.
   d. Determining syllabication.
   e. Using accents (primary and secondary).
   f. Using diacritical marks.
      (1) breve (short sound of vowel, at)
      (2) macron (long sound of vowel, ate)
      (3) modified macron (to designate a modified long sound.)
      (4) circumflex
      (5) breve circumflex
      (6) tilde
      (7) one dot above vowel
      (8) two dots above vowel

Reading as a Means of Cultivating Oral and Written Self-Expression

Advanced experience in semantics, usage and language structure received at this level makes possible the happy combination of fluency and polish which characterize good speech. Although the fifth grade pupil continues to remain by choice in the world of childhood and imagination, he is capable of communicating with the adult world in its own terms. The fifth grade pupil is fairly independent and self-sufficient as he clings to his chosen way of life and enjoys the activities of his selection, and at the same time he feels respect for, or at least admits tolerance of, the adult world. For just a little while now (two years at the most) he bears no resentment for nor grudges against his parents and teachers. He is happy being himself, and he has not found rebellion essential to self-fulfillment. His speech, therefore, is free and easy, whether he communicates with his classmates or with adults. This is the ripest time for establishing correct speech habits in an incidental manner. The adolescent will cling to his incorrect habits as a form of self-assertion;

the primary pupil will not have had enough formal instruction in usage to understand the reasoning behind the correction; the intermediate will be able to understand his error and will take the correction without offense and sometimes with amusement.

Language Structure. The fifth grade pupil should be well grounded in basic language structure. The structure and types of sentences should be known and recognizable, and he seldom should be guilty of composing an incomplete or basically incorrect sentence. The subject and predicate relationship should also be understood, and their agreement should be a conscious process in composition. Correct usage of adjectives and adverbs and continued attention to the right use of pronouns receive considerable emphasis. There is no excuse for the average fifth grade pupil who knows quite well what to say not to know how to say it. His knowledge of paragraphing, too, should be nearing perfection. Conscious attention to organization in the outlining process and to topic sentences in the skimming process do much toward establishing an awareness of the function of the paragraph and to the process of paragraphing.

Specific attention might well be directed to the first two sentences in the preceding paragraph. The fifth grade pupil cannot be expected to arrive in the fifth grade classroom demonstrating a high degree of perfection in all of the techniques enumerated. Regardless of how well he is prepared by his fourth grade teacher, he must be taught, told, and told again when he errs. He is ready to practice the many skills of usage, structure and semantics in speech and in writing, but the practice must be guided; he is not ready for private practice. Whenever possible, in group projects which demand oral and written contributions by individuals the teacher should call for the preparation of original drafts to be presented to her for correction before they are presented to the group or submitted in final form. This serves the dual purpose of calling the child's attention to his mistakes and inadequacies and avoiding the embarrassment of individuals in displaying their errors before the group. Some teachers, regardless of their actual beliefs, behave as if the goal of teaching were continual testing rather than a program of guided achievement. Permitting pupils to proceed somewhat independently and gain their "sea legs" is to be defended, but to withhold instruction and aid until they complete their erratic attempts at proficiency is going a bit too far.

When it is obvious to the teacher that an individual or a group is proceeding in an inefficient manner, it is time to state the need and instigate procedures to meet it. Correcting errors and calling them to the pupil's attention in the beginning is far better than waiting until mistakes have become established. Close observation is necessary to spot and correct errors in form or procedure, but despite the extra minutes required to execute a corrective program, it is in the long run the most conservative instructional process known. Recall that the words you will never be unsure of spelling are those you missed in spelling matches, and the questions to which you can give the most definite answers are those you failed to answer correctly on the test. To be certain and correct is commendable; to err and learn from one's mistakes is enlightening; to be uncertain of one's choices and to remain ignorant as to their corrections or incorrectness admits no advancement.

Pupils at this level have a great deal of use for oral and written expression. The continual emphasis upon use of references and organization of material is important in making of oral and written reports. Lucid, intelligent, coherent statements should be required in addition to structural, usage, and spelling accuracy. Individual correction and assistance in these areas should be as much a part of the planning and program as motivation, selection of activities, skill development, appreciation, and appraisal.

Creative Expression. The program must provide also for creative expression, which although requiring the accuracy, lucidity and intelligence of journalistic reporting, relies in addition upon the imagination, sense of beauty, and artistic arrangement for its effectiveness. Undeniably, pupils must learn to make reports and write business letters. They also must express themselves creatively in terms of inner feelings resulting from experiences with the world about them. This need — which is a need to communicate and to be understood — is universal. Writing talent is not universal, and yet the expression need not be superior or talented to be satisfying and accomplished. If the words are one's own and the appreciation of audience or readers is anticipated, talent and superiority may be discounted.

Endeavor first to teach pupils to make themselves understood. Putting feelings and experiences into words is the first hurdle and the essence of self-expression. This is something which everyone can attain through imitation, if in no other way, because feelings and experiences are somewhat universal. The child who employs this method of self-expression and meets with appreciation will have a satisfaction and a sense of accomplishment. He will not feel inadequate because a talented classmate speaks and writes more originally and entertainingly. He will merely appreciate excellence more for having attempted it and fallen short. An appreciation for line and color is not limited to the artist, nor is an appreciation for music limited to the musical; there are many persons who can recognize a tune although they are entirely incapable of reproducing it. Likewise, the reader who is without writing talent himself can show avid appreciation for great writing and can become an impeccable judge of literary quality.

To apply the theory outlined very practically some specific suggestions are in order. Creative efforts should, of course, grow out of needs and interests. Suppose the class is engaged in a project involving historical research. What would be more natural than to whet the imagination with the question, "Suppose I had lived then?" A story with a historical setting will be suggested to the more creative. To the less creative or the less motivated, exposure to fiction from the era under consideration will promote imaginative exercise and set a pattern for imitation. The creative motive will in turn inspire more meticulous research, wider reading and sympathetic understanding of the human predicament at the time in question. Feelings of patriotism, loyalty, appreciation, love, hate, fear, etc., may be aroused and find expression in poetry or inspired and beautiful prose. The consuming project may be life in another country. To write a description of natural scenery or the story of a boy or girl living in or touring the faraway place might be suggested. A concept of grandeur, charm or wonder in connection with the place might inspire a poem, as might the thought that it would be very undesirable to live in such a place or way! The wide realm of science fiction need not be mentioned. Once imaginations are fired — and they should be rather often — self-expression will result. The teacher then will have her work clearly outlined: to follow along, correcting, polishing, appreciating, and perhaps to get caught in the act herself.

Questions for Class Discussion

1. Discuss oral reading, its purposes and the practical ways a teacher might improve this skill.

2. How might a teacher change the attitude of a student who thinks poetry is something to be avoided?

3. How might a teacher provide for individual differences in a heterogenously grouped class?

4. Discuss the four classes of skill development needed to follow the meaning and thinking of the author.

5. Discuss remedial procedures which might be used to strengthen each of the four classes of skills mentioned in 4.

6. Why is it important for a teacher to have a comprehensive knowledge of children's literature?

Activities for Further Study

1. We know that students who are actively involved in a learning situation profit much more than those who are passive. Make a list of activities involving poetry in which your students might take part.

2. A bulletin board can be a very effective teaching-learning medium. Make a card file of possible ways it might be utilized

to enrich vocabulary. Sketch a small scale replica of the projected bulletin board on the card.

3. Trade books offer opportunities to teach concepts, attitudes and understandings. Can you suggest books for a fifth grade class — books that would deal with understanding self and others?

Suggested Classroom Materials

Story Collections:

ARBUTHNOT, MAY HILL (Compiler). *The Arbuthnot Anthology of Children's Literature.* Chicago: Scott, Foresman and Company, 1953.

FINGER, CHARLES (Compiler). *Tales From Silver Lands.* New York: Doubleday and Company, Inc., 1924.

HUBER, MIRIAM BLANTON (Editor). *Story and Verse for Children.* New York: The Macmillan Company, 1940.

Poetry Collections:

BENÉT, ROSEMARY, AND STEPHEN VINCENT. *A Book of Americans.* New York: Rinehart & Company, Inc., 1933.

HOLLOWELL, LILLIAN (Editor). *A Book of Children's Literature:* Revised Edition. New York: Rinehart & Company, Inc., 1950.

WITHERS, CARL (Compiler). *A Rocket in My Pocket.* New York: Henry Holt & Company, Inc., 1948.

Play Collections:

BURACK, A. S. *Plays.* Boston: Plays, Inc.

FIELD, RACHEL. *Patchwork Plays.* New York: Doubleday & Company, Inc.

Films and Filmstrips:

Encyclopedia Britannica Films, Inc., Wilmette, Illinois.
Enrichment Teaching Materials, New York, New York.
Eye Gate House, Inc., Jamaica, New York.
Jim Handy Organization, Detroit, Michigan.
McGraw-Hill Book Co., Inc., New York, New York.

Recordings:

Enrichment Records, New York, New York.
Newberry Award Records, New York, New York.
RCA Victor Division, Radio Corporation of America, Camden, New Jersey.

Recreational Reading:

McCloskey, Robert. *Homer Price*. New York: Viking, 1943.

Seredy, Kate. *Good Master*. New York: Viking, 1925.

Judson, Clara. *Abraham Lincoln: Friend of the People*. Illustrated by Robert Frankenberg. Chicago: Follett, 1950.

Henry, Marguerite. *Misty of Chincoteague*. Illustrated by Wesley Dennis. Skokie, Illinois: Rand McNally, 1947.

Selected Readings

Betzner, Jean, *Exploring Literature with Children*. New York: Bureau of Publications, Teachers College, Columbia University, 1943.

Darrow, Helen F., and Howes, Virgil M., *Approaches to Individualized Reading*. New York: Appleton-Century-Crofts, Inc., 1960.

Fadiman, Clifton, *The Lifetime Reading Plan*. Cleveland, Ohio: The World Publishing Co., 1958.

Goodlad, John I., and Anderson, Robert H., *The Nongraded Elementary School*. New York: Harcourt, Brace and Co., 1959.

Gray, William S., "Role of Group and Individualized Teaching in a Sound Reading Program," *The Reading Teacher*, XI (1957).

Gray, William S., "New Approaches to the Study of Interpretation in Reading," *Journal of Educational Research*, LII (October, 1958), 65-67.

Hester, Kathleen B., *Teaching Every Child to Read*. New York: Harper and Brothers, 1954.

Lamoreaux, L. A., and Lee, D. M., *Learning to Read Through Experience*. New York: Appleton-Century-Crofts, Inc., 1943.

McKim, Margaret G., *Guiding Growth in Reading*. New York: The Macmillan Company, 1955.

Murray, C. Merrill, "Selecting an Elementary School Dictionary," *Elementary English*, XXXIV (May, 1957), 293-97.

Piekarz, Josephine A., "Getting Meaning From Reading," *Elementary School Journal*, LVI (March, 1956), 303-9.

Veatch, Jeanette, *Individualizing Your Reading Program*. New York: G. P. Putnam's Sons, 1959.

THE TEACHING OF READING AT THE SIXTH GRADE LEVEL

CHAPTER 4

The sixth grade pupil reads a minimum of two hundred words per minute. He can read orally with intelligence material at his level which he has not read silently. He reads with expression, that is to say, he makes proper allowance for punctuation, conversation and attitude, but unless emotional and dramatic habits have been cultivated previously he will shy away from their use. His reading versatility is increasing. He can judge, with some independence in areas of familiarity, whether he should read carefully or merely skim to locate information and whether his purpose is to use the book as a reference tool or as a subject to master. He can consciously increase or decrease his reading speed to meet a need. When impatiently awaiting the solution to one of the mystery stories (which he regards very highly as a type of reading) he may increase his normal reading speed by fifty or more words per minute without sacrificing comprehension. In study-type reading he may read slowly, reread, attempt to organize and recall what he has read, check his memory by skimming the same passage, and so on. He is beginning to think more abstractly. Whereas formerly he has been *prompted* to infer, evaluate and examine, he now takes the initiative in the process to such an extent that he may occasionally confuse his teacher.

One teacher cites a personal experience during a study of Greek and Roman civilization in which her pupils questioned the worth of such a study to them, since, they said, their civilization was so completely different. Several pupils defended the study, pointing out that in our time great value is placed upon the contributions and works of art from the period in question. The teacher determined wisely to terminate the study temporarily until its worth could be established. Pupils would be allowed to select either side of the question and compile evidence to support their views. The following week the subject would be debated informally by the class. Obviously, the only means by which the supporting arguments could be established were by reading extensively about Greek and Roman civilization and examining our civilization for the evolutionary trace of Greek and Roman philosophy and government.

Experience with the use of reference materials indicated that the pupils were in need of instruction in finding them in the library, locating relevant material within a given source, note-taking, outlining, skimming, and making a bibliography. A lecture to the entire group by the librarian, followed by personal assistance by the teacher and the librarian, proved to be of definite benefit. Language and reading exercises in skimming, outlining, note-taking, preparing bibliographies, locating information quickly from tables of contents and indexes were selected and prepared by the teacher. The need for them was already established as a result of the history project, so they were well received and conscientiously applied during the history period also. Progress in the final outcome was observable in the independent use of the library including the card catalog, standard reference materials, selection of related information, skimming, note-taking, outlining, organization of material from various sources for a specific purpose, criticism and critical thinking in relation to the pupils' own views and the views of others.

Such experiences should make every teacher and prospective teacher extremely aware of the necessity to work within the classroom situation, guiding while following the interests of the group rather than making arbitrary assignments and autocratic rules. More than a few teachers might have yielded in the foregoing situation to the temptation to defend the study, to point out convincingly (to themselves) its worth and then to proceed with it. Their pupils, lukewarm and poorly motivated in relation to the study, would actually have been content with much less information and would have gained nothing in the realm of reading and language skills as outlined. It is more difficult and much less perfunctory for a teacher to create or to permit her pupils to create a learning situation than it is to impart information to them or to assign material which will do so. The good teacher will scrap her lesson plans when imagination, spontaneity and opportunity offer something as good as or superior to what she had planned. She will then remain alert to needs and interests, capitalizing upon them to teach more effectively what she would have taught anyway.

Reading as a Mental Process

Skills of Interpretation. The refinement of the skills can be given unequivocally as the most vital aspect of the mental process of reading at the sixth grade level. The good sixth grade reader is constantly seeking to find answers, to solve problems and to satisfy mental and emotional needs through reading. His ability to interpret what he reads therefore has a direct and significant bearing upon the progress he makes in these areas and finally upon his general achievement.

Interpretation involves a number of abilities which must be developed or perfected at this level, and one of the most important of these is *comprehension,* which has remained near the top since its first major emphasis at the second grade level. There are many methods of estimating comprehension. A sure method of gauging it (and one which should be employed during the sixth grade reading program) is a good standardized test which measures accurately the degree and level of comprehension and other essential factors. Pupils should have experience in interpreting what they read silently, what they read orally, and what is read to them. Direct questions and open discussions will reveal any interpretations which result from inadequate understanding or unintelligent consideration of the content. Most sixth grade pupils are fairly proficient in comprehension of material at or below their reading level. Reading guides in the form of questions, statements, or notes written on the blackboard aid in comprehension because they direct specific attention to those points which insure it. These, of course, are continued as artificial means of forcing a process which can be achieved naturally as a result of motivation of interest and curiosity.

Critical analysis of material read is the second element of interpretation which needs refining. Sixth grade pupils have not read so widely and discriminatingly that they can be confident of the validity of content, nor have they adequate means of checking upon the reputations and reliability of authors. In certain areas of critical analysis, however, and to some extent, pupils should be adept at considering validity and reliability of material.

1. They should certainly be able, for instance, to look at the copyright date in a reference book, and thereby to appraise scientific information for current reliability. Similarly, they should reject a history book copyrighted in 1940 as a source of information about World War II.

2. The possibility of a firsthand account's being an actual experience of the author should be observed. Fantastic or improbable events should discredit this hypothesis.

3. Cross references should be noted and checked.

4. Pupils should know what references, if they are up-to-date, are at all times considered reliable.

5. There should be an evaluation of the material upon the basis of each pupil's own experience, including his previous reading. Pupils should be aware, however, that this experience is limited and subject to broadening and intensification.

6. At least a beginning should be made in discovering bias or prejudice in an author. In other words, the pupil should know definitely when the author is stating an absolute fact and when he is giving a distorted or one-sided account. Conflicting editorials from different newspapers are an excellent means of demonstrating this. Viewing the same factual situation from two differing opinions often leads to the conclusion that the indisputable facts have suffered some alteration in one or both viewpoints.

These critical abilities cannot be molded into the mental make-up of sixth grade pupils, nor can pupils be expected to reveal the same amount of discrimination as they will achieve at the senior high school level. The sixth grade teacher can, however, by insisting upon proper acknowledgment of sources, checking of references and intelligent appraisal of information, create in the sixth grade pupil an awareness of his responsibility to read with open eyes, open-mindedness and a modicum of experiential interpretation. With the present use of mass media, including television, in advertising and politics, the teacher obviously must help the students develop awareness of propaganda, bias, and misleading statements in materials other than books.

Reading as a Communicative Process

Printed pages "speak" to the sixth grade pupil. Highly developed reading skills enable a practiced performance in reading even unfamiliar material or new subject matter. The vocabulary is much larger as a result of technical words common to the different subject fields and as a result of wide reading and the consequent familiarity with a greater variety of words. The reading process thus is not interrupted or rendered less effective because of vocabulary deficiency. The enlarging background of reading serves simultaneously as a springboard to vaster experiences and as a foil against which the marvels of rapidly increasing knowledge are displayed. The sixth grade pupil has reached the authoritative stage in some fields. Many sixth grade boys are virtual experts in the fields of aviation, navigation, space travel, etc. Budding collections of various types and creative and practical hobbies among boys and girls have inspired specialized interests and specialized reading.

The instructional process in communication at this stage is twofold and paradoxical. On the one hand, the teacher must guard against overzealousness in supervision of the reading program to permit independence in location and selection of material. On the other hand, she must not permit flights of fancy into all directions at once to preclude correlation of the program and of group interests and to foster a helter-skelter attitude which defies all of the laws of learning. Fortunately, both goals can be accomplished. An awareness that learning must proceed from the known to the unknown, from the simple to the complex, and that for best results it must be motivated by curiosity and sustained by interest is the essential knowledge required to perform the task. Guidance and supervision then can be confined to the realms of motivation, selection of projects or areas of learning and evaluation of outcomes, while the entire, wonderful realm of independent discovery can remain unmolested and sometimes uninfluenced by outside suggestion. The teacher holds the reins in such a program. She may close her eyes, but when she does she is certain that the horse knows the way back home.

The Discovery Method.   To illustrate the method described, let us suppose that the group is about to study China. To stimulate interest in discovering facts about China and as a basis for reference reading, a problem or an objective must be stated. The exact slant should grow out of the interest of the group, since whatever character the problem assumes will serve to promote the general end of acquiring considerable information about the geography, history, civilization, culture and government of China. Perhaps the group will become interested in China's present political situation and will express the problem in this manner. Exactly what is China's present political position, and what factors have promoted or created it? The information which is already known can then be discussed and noted on the blackboard. Such items as these might be listed:

1. Communism controls the Chinese mainland.
2. The Chinese Nationalists under Chiang-Kai-Shek have long held American sympathy.
3. China is heavily populated, and her people live on a low economic level.
4. China is a very large country.
5. China is not advanced industrially.

Following the list of known factors, the group should select and state the specific questions or points which will yield the desired information. This list should be made by the group with as little teacher direction as possible. Questions might be somewhat like the following:

1. What has been China's political history over the past hundred years?
2. What are the main problems of the Chinese people?
3. What are their chief resources and natural assets?
4. How does the thinking of the Chinese differ from ours?
5. What factors from the past have contributed to present Chinese characteristics and outlook?
6. What has been the recent attitude of China in world affairs, and what effects has it had?

The sources in which such information can be found should be listed by the group to guide the pupils in their use of reference materials. (Some pupils will discover additional materials which will be posted as references, and publications can be ordered from the United Nations. Collected back copies of *My Weekly Reader,*[1] newspaper and other magazine articles can be skimmed for pertinent information. *The Reader's Guide to Periodical Literature*[2] can be introduced at this point.) The plan

---

[1]*My Weekly Reader.* Columbus, Ohio: American Education Publications.
[2]*The Reader's Guide to Periodical Literature.* New York: The H. W. Wilson Company.

of attack can then be formulated. The decision to work individually or in groups must be made, and the form which the collected information will take must be determined. Oral reports, discussions, booklets, displays, art projects, etc., are among the possibilities. Details of the approach and execution of the project, if it is to be meaningful, must be determined by a group evaluation of the information and accomplishments in relation to the originally stated aims of the study or questions.

From the standpoint of developing communicative skills, selectivity of subject matter is not a deterrent. To receive the information and ideas regarding selected topics the mind must be open to divergent points of view, implications, and inconsistencies. The communicative process remains virtually unchanged, with selection confined to subject matter rather than to reading technique.

Oral Reading. The sixth grade pupil can give an intelligent oral reading without preparation merely by reading the material so that it makes sense to him. The past injunction which has been "Read with expression, so that everyone can get the meaning" now is revised "Read for meaning, so that your reading will contain expression." This is not the total oral reading picture, but it is an increasingly important aspect of it as more reference and report reading of an expository nature is necessary. This type of reading usually is noncontroversial in attitude, and is almost never dramatic or emotional. Its sole aim is to enlighten, and it is frequently introduced into a discussion spontaneously and without time for preparation. It is presented purposefully in a meaningful situation, and, because of the attention focused upon it, does not forfeit its communicative effect for an occasional mispronunciation. Good *grouping* of words, sufficient *pausing* at the proper points and clear *enunciation* are the primary skills involved in this type of oral reading. Pupils who have difficulty reading phrases at a glance, making allowance for punctuation and speaking clearly and distinctly should receive individual, corrective instruction in the areas of difficulty, preferably without an audience.

The other types of oral reading formerly described as a method of sharing entertaining reading selections continue to receive a place in the reading program. Preparation, rehearsal and polished performance should continue to be emphasized in this type of reading assignment. In most cases, such readings will not be required frequently because the sixth grade pupil has attained a reading ease which permits him to read intelligently and well without a great deal of attention to either the mechanics or the dramatics. There should, however, be sufficient attention to continue the habit of reading with expression for the purpose of entertainment. An excellent practice is to have several tape recordings for each pupil during the school term. After the reading the teacher's corrections and criticism should also be recorded and the entire tape played back, so that the pupil will be listening to his errors with the intention of correcting them. When this procedure is used interest is increased, and wherever interest exists, maximum achievement is insured. A pupil who prepares a two-minute reading every three or four weeks and presents it in an audience situation will receive more training in form, presentation and mechanical elements of voice, pitch, enunciation and expression than he actually needs. The surplus, however, will be an investment in poise, self-confidence, dramatic ability, self-satisfaction, sense of identification with others and perception of audience reaction, any of which may sometime prove valuable, if not vital.

Reading as a Pleasurable Process

Numerous surveys reveal that the average child reading at the sixth grade level has an appreciation for the literature which educated adults pronounce good and great. Pupils at this stage select and read independently for pleasure such books as *Treasure Island, Robinson Crusoe, Tom Swift, Black Beauty, The Adventures of Tom Sawyer, Little Women, Heidi, Alice in Wonderland, Robin Hood, Pilgrim's Progress,* and *The Tale of Two Cities.* These titles appear on lists of favorites among sixth grade boys and girls, and, as might be expected, alternate with mystery and adventure series and less established works. The diverse interests of sixth grade pupils and their more mature concept of events and human reactions combine to create a desire for many types of reading and an ability to understand the intricate plots and situations, mature emotions, adult reactions, and sophisticated themes. Again the foremost consideration is that the sixth grade pupil should read avidly, and in this he generally requires no prodding. His curiosity about life, his desire for knowledge and experience in living, and the budding necessity to "lose himself" or to "escape" make reading a naturally satisfying experience.

For the few who do not read eagerly the example of their classmates and a literary discussion period held once or twice a week are strong incentives. When a favorite book of literary worth has passed from one member of the class to another until almost everyone has read it, or when teacher or pupils have read such a book orally serial-fashion to the entire group, discussion of the characters, situations and ideas is a natural and rewarding experience and a strong incentive to further reading. Many times the teacher can allude casually to another plot or character of which she is reminded, and by a few well-chosen words can arouse an interest in reading another great book. Although the majority of sixth grade pupils will read enough of the great along with the good and mediocre which libraries offer, the teacher can encourage a tendency toward an appreciation for the better if she suggests subtly, guides casually, and arouses curiosity to the point that the less palatable initial 150 pages are read in order to have the proper background for the tantalizing pages that remain.

For reading aloud to the class, *Arabian Nights, Gulliver's Travels* and quite a few Shakespearean plays rewritten well in story form are near the sixth grade level and can be read by individual pupils who read well. These stories have high entertainment value when read well and lend themselves to discussions which can be speculative, philosophical, individually helpful in fostering desirable attitudes and outlook, and collectively beneficial in creating group unity and better pupil-teacher and pupil-class relationships. *Homer* and *Virgil* can be read from translation by the teacher or in rewritten form by pupils. The age of knighthood and romance is in the height of its appeal, and King Arthur will be well received in the prose versions or in the poetry of Tennyson.

In poetry some of Wordsworth, Byron, Shelly, and Keats, much of Tennyson, Longfellow and Whitman, all of Whittier, and numerous good poems by lesser poets will be understood, enjoyed and reread until memorized. Seasonal poems and nature poetry are very popular, and narrative poetry is high in appeal if the story is meaty. The robust, rollicking songs of the sea, the atmospheric or mood poems with a touch of whimsy, the sentimental longings, the humorous, the grotesque — all are enjoyed. The teacher's desire to present such poetry to the group and her ability to read it will have a marked effect upon its reception. Many excellent recordings of poetry read by living or late authors or by actors and actresses are available, and the little time required to play them in the classroom is a wise investment in future appreciation.

Reading as a Process Requiring the Development and Perfection of Many Skills

From the basic word recognition skills to the highest levels of abstraction involved in semantic analysis the sixth grade program must provide specific opportunities for development and perfection of reading skills. The program must be well ordered and clearly defined on the one hand, and on the other flexible enough to permit adaptation of instructional procedures to incidental classroom activities and projects and units of study. The program of skill development must accommodate itself to the learning situation.

From the teaching standpoint this means that an understanding and knowledge of the scope and elements of the skill program must be a conscious reality. In addition the habit of examining every activity, project, unit, and reading situation for opportunities to develop skills in a pertinent, interesting, related manner must be fixed. From the learning standpoint such instructional forethought and relevancy mean conservation of time and materials, immediate interest as a result of the connection with a previously motivated activity, and opportunity for practical application which demonstrates the value of the skill in question. Very practically, a teacher must examine carefully the scope of the technical skills for which she is responsible and must be asking herself constantly: In what area of skill development can this activity or unit or project provide application? She must also consider immediate needs of the group, anticipating them, recognizing them and providing for their satisfaction.

The skills program at the sixth grade level is comprehensive. Word recognition, including structural analysis skills, phonics, and context clues, must be well established. The phonics skills are integrated with dictionary skills as a practical expedient whenever possible, but they may be separated for analysis. The rules for vowel sounds in open and closed syllables, and vowels followed by r, are examples of the use of phonics at the sixth grade level. Context clues as provided by appositives, implications, contrasting ideas and anticipation of familiar expressions receive attention. The teacher can take a cue here from the scientific design of textual materials, occasionally injecting into her classroom speech words unfamiliar to her pupils with *appositional explanation* or clues of *implication* or *contrast*. (Examples:)

1. Persiflage, flattery, is sometimes hard to recognize. Appositional definition.
2. Because of his many insincere compliments she decided he was inclined toward persiflage. Implication.

3. Persiflage can often be distinguished from an honest compliment. Contrast. Structural analysis skills, (especially syllabication principles for specific skills to emphasize at the sixth grade level), prefixes, suffixes, contractions and possesssives must be

developed and perfected. Inductive statement of rules and deductive application constitute the wisest procedure in instruction in this area, insuring meaningfulness of the rules and immediate application. Observing that one writes *girl's dress* but *girls' dresses* leads to the induction of the rule that singular nouns form their possessives by the addition of an apostrophe and an s, and plural nouns ending in s form their possessives by adding only an apostrophe. The pupil who follows the inductive thinking process can immediately apply it deductively to such problems as the *animal nose* and the *animals' noses.*

Versatility in reading becomes increasingly important, and the sixth grade pupil should be able to decide when presented with an assignment what type of reading will be required. To skim, to study, to read quickly, to locate information, to read critically, etc., should be fairly simple decisions. The teacher will continue to state the reading purpose frequently when the class or a group is reading the same material for the same purpose, and the statement should leave no doubt in the mind of the pupil as to the type of reading he should employ. Much research and reference work required by study units will be independent and individual activity, but even in this type of reading the pupil should have either his own clearly defined purpose or a group-selected purpose which is meaningful to him and which implies to him a certain method or procedure in achieving an immediate goal.

Organization of material continues to be a frequently needed skill, and any sixth grade pupil, building upon his ability to identify one or more main ideas, to observe sequence, and to determine the relevance of details, should be able to grasp the procedure of outlining and utilize it in organizing material. Here, too, there should be experience in concentrating material into outline form and in writing or summarizing from the outline. Note-taking and outlining should be a means rather than an end to the sixth grade pupil. The procedures should be adapted easily to the material considered. Application of these techniques under observation will reveal insufficient experience with the forms or the need for corrective or instructional procedures.

The sixth grade is not actually a point of no return, because each successive teacher will be expected to institute corrective procedures indicated by testing and observation. The sixth grade teacher should be definitely aware, however, that at the junior high school level increased attention will be given to applying the skills which adequate instruction and practice should have developed. The ability to use books effectively is the greatest asset which can be brought to the junior high school, and the sixth grade teacher should be certain that she has provided sufficient experience with the encyclopedia, dictionary, atlas, card catalogue, Reader's Guide, etc., as well as with tables of contents, indexes, glossaries, maps, charts, and graphs.

Reading as a Means of Cultivating Oral and Written Self-Expression

Improvement of the *vocabulary* is the most obvious result of the sixth grade reading program. At the sixth grade level, pupils become acquainted with many technical words and the opening vistas of pleasure reading introduce many previously unused but understood words which are added to the speaking vocabulary. General conversational and discussion abilities show marked improvement with the increase in vocabulary, and the ease with which ideas and thoughts are expressed facilitates communication by insuring proper reception of the exact shade of meaning intended by the speaker. This, in turn, gives the speaker greater confidence, and his increased self-assurance stimulates even greater speaking fluency.

The time is ripe, therefore, for practical application in all of the areas of self-expression. There should be a "last call" for perfection in *correct usage,* and with the many opportunities for discussion, oral reporting, and writing afforded to all, the teacher will have ample occasion to make note of any individual errors or group weaknesses which develop or persist. Agreement in

Improved Vocabulary (a) + Correct Usage (b) + Condensation of the Material (c) + Whipping It Into Form (d) = Creative Power (e)

number of subject and predicate, pronoun cases, and irregular verbs will be high on the list for corrective procedures. Despite the adequate experience provided in these areas by most study books and worktexts in reading and language arts, there is no substitute for immediate recognition and correction of errors. Formal instruction is reliable to the extent of its observable effectiveness, but one (and perhaps one hundred) formal instruction periods in usage will not accomplish as much for an individual as the incidental and consistent correction and explanation of his errors.

Rewording and condensing material read is not the highest form of self-expression but it is a much used method in teaching the reading skills of organization, remembering details, getting the main idea, and recalling sequence. It should also be subject to the best standards of usage, form and artistic expression. Careful choice of words, clarity of expression, and attractive and interesting presentation even in repetition are worthy goals, and insistence upon accurate and interesting reports brings rewards in other fields and areas to which the habit is transferred.

Form itself should receive attention. Any sixth grade pupil without reference materials or means of checking should be able to compose in the proper form an interesting friendly letter, a concise business letter, a summary or résumé, an outline, a book review, a brief theme or essay, a story, a play, or a poem. This is not to say that the last three mentioned should show literary promise; it is only to say that the form of each should be so well known that it can be reproduced correctly from memory.

The poem might show no appreciation for meter, rhyme, or esthetic expression, but it should be written in lines rather than in sentences with the first letter of each line capitalized (since most sixth graders have yet to encounter e e cummings).[3] The story should have a plot, characters, climax and conclusion, and it should be written in paragraphs with proper respect for quotations and punctuation. That it is devoid of interest, insight and

---

[3]Cummings, Edward Estin.

artistry is not a major concern at this point. The play form should be used rather extensively at the sixth grade level as an organizational method in rewriting stories. Such skills as getting the main idea, remembering details, and sequence, and frequently note-taking, outlining and summarizing are expanded in this type of writing.

Beyond these, the *critical skills* of observation, sympathy, vicarious participation, understanding through thinking oneself into a situation, judgment and appraisal are called into play. In another vein the skills of diction, usage, spelling, punctuation and sentence structure are improved. Most far-reaching of all, the *creative powers* of artistic expression and insight are sometimes tapped in such a way that a child will "lose himself" (or "find himself" if you prefer) in the wonderful world of conjecture and imaginative discovery which culminuates in self-discovery and fulfillment. Always for some and sometime for all there must be opportunity for creativity, for introspection, for the world of mental delving which finds meaning in existence and gives existence to meaning. Sixth grade pupils are ready for exposure to life-size situations and they should be encouraged to confront them with mental strength, fortitude and resoluteness. It is through this type of response that self-expression comes, and it is through self-expression that the personality is fulfilled.

QUESTIONS FOR CLASS DISCUSSION

1. How might a teacher capitalize on interests in the sixth grade?
2. What informal procedures might a teacher use in evaluating comprehension?
3. Why is it so vitally important for the sixth grade student to have a solid background of upper level reading skills?
4. How might the library actually be utilized as a learning laboratory?
5. Discuss reading skills that might be developed or strengthened in sixth grade.
6. Why is guidance so necessary in written self-expression?

ACTIVITIES FOR FURTHER STUDY

1. Have students plan a radio skit to strengthen oral reading skills, or have them record on tape their oral interpretation of a favorite prose passage or poem. Personal evaluations could follow.

2. Obtain recordings of poetry done by such people as Sandburg, Frost, etc. After students have heard recordings, let them discuss the most appealing aspect.

3. Designate a particular day in the week as "word day." Have each student in your class present a new word to the class, tell its meaning and use it in a sentence. During that day, the students might try to use that word in their speaking vocabulary.

SUGGESTED CLASSROOM MATERIALS

Story Collections:

GÁG, WANDA (Translator). *Tales from Grimm*. New York: Coward-McCann, Inc., 1926.

GRUENBERG, SIDONIE M. (Editor). *Favorite Stories Old and New*: Revised Edition. New York: Doubleday & Company, Inc., 1955.

KIPLING, RUDYARD. *The Jungle Books*: Two volumes. New York: Doubleday & Company, Inc., 1948.

———. *New Illustrated Just So Stories*. New York: Garden City Books, 1952.

Poetry Collections:

BREWTON, SARA AND JOHN E. *Bridled with Rainbows*. Macmillan.

RICHARDS, LAURA E. *Tirra-Lirra*. Boston: Little, Brown & Company, 1955.

Plays:

FIELD, RACHEL. *Patchwork Plays*. New York: Doubleday & Company, Inc.

STEVENSON, AUGUSTA. *A Hole in the Dike, and Other Plays*. Boston: Houghton Mifflin.

Films and Filmstrips:

Academic Film Co., Inc., New York, New York.

Film Images, Inc., New York, New York.

Ford Motor Co., Dearborn, Michigan.

Life Filmstrips, New York, New York.

NET Film Service, Bloomington, Indiana.

Visual Education Consultants, Inc., Madison, Wisconsin.

Recordings:

Caedmon Publishers, New York, New York.

Cornell University Records, Cornell University Press, Ithaca, New York.

Greystone Press, New York, New York.

Recreational Readings:

DEANGELI, MARGUERITE. *Door in the Wall.* New York: Doubleday, 1949.

ESTES, ELEANOR. *The Moffats.* Harcourt.

FORBES, ESTHER. *Johnny Tremain.* Illustrated by Lynd Ward. Boston: Houghton, 1943.

KJELGAARD, JAMES. *Big Red.* Holiday.

KRUMGOLD, JOSEPH. *Onion John.* New York: Crowell, 1959.

NORTON, MARY. *The Borrowers.* Harcourt.

RAWLINGS, MARJORIE K. *The Yearling.* Illustrated by N. C. Wyeth. New York: Scribners, 1939.

ROBINSON, MABEL L. *Bright Island.* Random House.

SELECTED READINGS

ARBUTHNOT, MAY H. *The Arbuthnot Anthology.* Chicago: Scott, Foresman, 1961.

BERRY, JUNE, AND MERCER, WINSTON. "Developing Library Skills — Every Teacher's Responsibility," *Education,* LXXVIII (October, 1957), 78-81.

BLOOMFIELD, LEONARD, AND BARNHART, CLARENCE L. *Let's Read — A Linguistic Approach.* Detroit: Wayne University Press, 1961.

CENTER, STELLA. *The Art of Book Reading.* New York: Charles Scribner's Sons, 1953.

CHALL, JEANNE. "The Encyclopedia as an Educational Tool," *Teachers College Record* (February, 1961).

FITZGERALD, BURDETTE S. *World Tales for Creative Dramatics and Storytelling.* Englewood Cliffs, N. J.: Prentice-Hall, 1962.

GATES, ARTHUR I. *The Improvement of Reading.* New York: The Macmillan Co., 1947.

HILLENBRAND, ROBERT. "The Appreciation of Picturesque Language in the Intermediate Grades," *Elementary English*, XXXVI (May, 1959), 302-4.

HUCK, CHARLOTTE S., AND YOUNG, DORIS. *Children's Literature in the Elementary School*. New York: Holt, Rinehart, and Winston, 1961.

INHELDER, BARBEL, AND PIAGET, JEAN. *The Growth of Logical Thinking*. New York: Basic Books, 1958.

JACOBS, LELAND B. "Historical Fiction for Children," *The Reading Teacher* (January, 1961), 191-94.

LESTON, CHARLES T. "Speed and Comprehension in Reading," *Journal of Educational Research*, L11 (October, 1958), 49-53.

NARDELLI, ROBERT R. "Some Aspects of Creative Reading," *Journal of Educational Research*, L (March, 1957), 495-508.

PRESTON, RALPH C., AND BOTEL, MORTON. *How to Study*. Chicago: Science Research Associates, Inc., 1957.

SMITH, NILA B. "Teaching Study Skills in Reading," *Elementary School* Journal, LX (December, 1959), 158-62.

SOCHOR, E. ELONA, et al. *Critical Reading*: An Introduction. Champaign, Ill.: National Council of Teachers of English, 1959.

CHAPTER 5

THE REMEDIAL PROGRAM

The preceding chapters have described and illustrated the processes through which pupil masters the reading process. Unfortunately, as is shown by the evidence in the literature, the well-publicized criticism in the press, and the multitude of college courses, workshops, and clinics, many children fail to master the process to their fullest capacities. The term "remedial reading" is commonly associated with the attempts of the teacher to provide a program that will encourage all pupils needing help to read to the best of their abilities. In terms of the processes involved, remedial reading is no different from any other kind of reading, since the techniques used are the same as would be employed in an efficient presentation of any new level of instruction. The major difficulty is that children who need remedial teaching, i.e., have not grasped the significance of the process at first encounter, have, as a result of failure, often become insecure and developed emotional problems as well as reading problems. The problem in remedial programs therefore often becomes twofold; first, the necessity of vitalizing and clarifying the process, and second, of building new confidence and overcoming aversion to reading.

Disability in Reading

The reading ability of a child should, and usually will, parallel the mental age. When the reading age, as measured by valid tests, is less than the mental age, the child is not reading to capacity and can be regarded as generally retarded in reading. The degree of retardation is of course the important factor to be considered, since a relatively wider disparity is to be expected as the child progresses through the levels of reading. Slight disparities between the comparative factors are usually not important in indicating need for remedial training but may be the sign of a more specific reading disability and should be carefully charted.

Reading disability cannot be accounted for simply on the basis of intelligence and cannot be predicted on that basis since a child with a relatively low intelligence quotient is classified as a "slow learner" and not a remedial case. In addition, due to the arbitrary nature of the graded structure, failure to read on a particular grade level at a particular chronological age does not necessarily indicate reading disability. Mental maturity is, however, a prerequisite for learning to read well and serves as the basis for studying progress of children. When it happens, for example, that a sixth grade boy with a mental maturity of 11 years and 7 months shows an 11 year ability in reading-age equivalent, we are satisfied that he is not a remedial case. Had that same boy attained an age equivalent of only ten years, however, he would logically be selected for remedial treatment. Another remedial case might be a 12 year old girl with a mental age of 14 years, 9 months, who has a reading age of 12 years, even though she might be reading on-grade material. Generally speaking, and when dealing with intermediate grade children, teachers must be prepared to offer remedial help when the relationship between mental age and reading age shows a retardation factor of a year or more.

Selection of Remedial Readers.   Probably the most used method of selecting readers for remedial work is the employment of data from general achievement tests, intelligence tests, diagnostic tests, and tests of capacities. When a reading test and an intelligence test have been given by a well-trained individual (more than once and of several types in case of doubt) a comparison of results can be the basis for determining the cases in need of remedial training. In addition, an informal testing program using graded material can aid in determining reading age. It must be emphasized that more than the results of a reading test are essential because such a test alone could be compared to only the grade level attained by the individual. This often leads to a mistaken interpretation, especially in the case of slow learners. The test to determine mental age is absolutely essential also. In addition, if results are available from achievement tests in other subjects, a more definite analysis can be made of the difficulty. For example, Tommy, a sixth grade boy with a mental age of 12, made an age equivalent score of 14 in arithmetic computation, 10 in reading, and 10 in spelling. Further study revealed the difficulty centered in his vocabulary development. Large differences in the test scores are certain to be significant. It also must be accepted that, valid or not, the school grade placement of the individual must be recognized as a factor.

Summarizing, then, reading disability cannot be assumed by a perfunctory inspection, cannot be assumed by failure to meet grade standards (or by success in meeting grade standards), but must be determined by careful consideration of chronological age, mental age, school grade, scores on reading tests, scores on other subject tests, reading rate, visual perception, and any health data available.

Causes of Reading Disability. The failure of a child to reach his capacity seldom is caused by one single factor but more often by a multiplicity of factors. To attempt to list all possible factors would of course by a never-ending task. The major causes can be identified, however, and would include:

1. Physical conditions including defective hearing or speech, poor eyesight, poor health, illness, poor kinesthetic sense, limited maturation, and lack of coordination.
2. Pedagogical reasons, including inadequate instructional materials, faulty teaching situations, limited motivation,

The Poor Reader's Disability; It May Be (a) Physical,
(b) Pedagogical, (c) Environmental, (d) Mental, or
(e) Poor Habits

lack of stimulation, and failure of the school to establish readiness.

3. Environmental cases, including emotional upsets, poor school attendance, broken homes, poor home conditions (food, sleep inadequate), little parental interest, and general discrediting influence and attitude of all concerned.

4. Mental situations, including varying degrees of intelligence, mental age, natural ability, limited maturation, awareness, stability, and self-conflicts.

5. Diagnostically incorrect habits, such as vocalization, errors in eye movements, and word-for-word reading.

Diagnostic Study

The identification of the pupil in need of remedial help is only the first, and often the less difficult, step in the remedial program. The next phase involves a carefully planned diagnostic study in an attempt to locate the difficulty or difficulties. There can be no step-by-step listing of diagnostic procedures but each of the following methods should be part of the repertoire of the skilled teacher.

Observation. As a method of studying children, this procedure is valuable for a variety of reasons and can be adopted to fit the situation. It is not limited to a particular time or place but can be utilized in the classroom, on the playground, and, in fact, under almost any natural condition. The teacher is able to observe personality traits and social position as well as formal work habits. Behavior symptoms to be particularly noted in dealing with reading disability would include:

1. Scholarship habits in groups of subjects.
2. Health and physical conditions.
3. Hearing, vision, and speech.
4. Social behavior.
5. Social acceptance.

Several pertinent points must be kept in mind when observing any child. The teacher must not guess or take conditions for granted; any trait or symptom must be observed many times and proven to be a factor before a procedure of correction can be started. In addition, because the teacher's memory is not infallible, careful notes should be made for later comparison against tested situations. John may show an unusual interest in a particular phase of nature study on a field trip which may be the very catalyst to spark his diminishing interest in reading. In the hustle of the trip, however, a nonobservant teacher could easily allow this bit of information to slide away into obscurity.

Anecdotal Record. Careful observations of a child's daily activities contribute valuable information. In order to give a more complete picture of the total child, however, the most significant episodes or acts should be recorded. The acts usually are termed anecdotes and their recording can be detailed under two major headings:

1. Behavior description. From observation of the child, the teacher will soon notice particular acts or events which seem to characterize him. When these events are recorded and described, an impartial picture of the life of the child begins to form. Once more, there must be a caution that there can be no inference or guesswork — only actual facts should be recorded. The teacher does not decide what is wrong with the child and then cite facts to prove it. Rather the cumulated record itself points the way to the problem and, optimistically, to the solution.

2. Interpretation. No matter how complete any record, it is useless unless properly interpreted. While it is not necessary to interpret every action, one plan would be to group similar events and to interpret them as to cause, importance, and possible remedial suggestions. The interpretation *is not* a part of the anecdotal record but part of the follow-up. Before attempting interpretations, certain points must be kept in mind, including:

a. Was it a natural behavior?
b. What caused it to take place?
c. Where and when?
d. Did the child know the teacher was watching?
e. Was this an individual action or was it part of a group action?

Interview. By talking with a child and allowing him to express himself, a more complete understanding is achieved, by the teacher and the child, of the problems involved. If the child understands his situation, a much more efficient and satisfactory program can be initiated. Not all teachers have success in "interviewing" a child, possibly because they fail to realize that the child should do the talking. The key to success with this method is the establishment of rapport and confidence and making certain that the child understands that guidance is of value to his attempt to master the process of reading. The interview method of getting to the problem is of particular value at the intermediate level and a sympathetic teacher can gain much by this technique. The contents for the interview depend upon the child, the problem, and the objective of the interview.

Home Environment Inventory. It is impossible to understand any child, and particularly one with problems, without knowing what situations he encounters when he goes home and the type of life he lives there. No child remains unaffected by home environment that includes such conditions as parental strife, poor family grouping, inferior surroundings, and lack of training. Since a better knowledge of these factors is essential, the teacher might utilize any or all of the following procedures.

1. Observe the child, considering type of lunch brought, clothes worn, attitude in the morning, willingness to take home notes on school functions, general appearance, and attendance.

2. Interview the child, talking about his leisure activities, recreation, and hobbies, leading him, professionally and ethically, into a discussion of his home life and family circle.

3. Invite the parents to school, discussing the program of remediation with them, and establishing a basis for further relationships.

4. Visit the home, preferably after an invitation, observing the environment, evidences of problems, and parent-child relationship.

Standardized Tests. In addition to the personal and more informal methods of studying the child, the utilization of standardized tests will help complete the picture. Such tests are more objective in pointing out certain facets, are often more reliable because of their nonpersonal nature, and afford a basis of comparison on a wide scale. A simplified list of desirable tests would include:

1. Intelligence tests. The child's basic ability must be known in order that the teacher will be able to judge more accurately what can be expected. Tests to determine intelligence have always been the fundamental instrument used in predicting the individual's capacity to make progress in reading. Reading experts have recognized, however, that group intelligence tests, because of the reading ability required, cannot be used as more than an indicator of possible disability. Whenever the teacher's estimate of the child's potential is in disagreement with the group intelligence test scores, or when a severe disability is indicated, the utilization of an individual intelligence test is recommended.

2. Survey tests. Group reading tests are generally of a "survey" nature in that they give an estimate of the reading level and the range of reading ability in a specific group. Generally these group tests measure reading abilities in vocabulary and comprehension.

3. Diagnostic tests. In order to determine as definitely as possible the amount and kind of remedial instruction needed and to locate specific weaknesses, the teacher needs to use such a scale. The standardized diagnostic test will supplement the teacher's own informal reading inventory.

4. Tests of reading speed. The teacher needs to be able to ascertain how rapidly the child is able to read with comprehension. Although tests in this category have been criticized because they penalize the slow student, they do add another measure to the diagnostic procedure.

Case-Study. All five of the factors of diagnostic study listed are essential if a complete analysis is to be made of the child and his reading disability. The material collected must be organized into a concise, easily used document or case study. An outline to summarize the suggested procedure is presented here as a guide. The number of steps followed and the amount of material to be included will depend upon the capability of the teacher and the nature of the problem involved.

1. Identification of the Problem.
   a. Observation
   b. Interview
   c. Analysis of test results
   d. Parental-school visits
   e. Teacher-home visits
   f. Description of child behavior

2. Developmental History
   a. Family history from visits, interviews
   b. Personal history from health record, family records, observations, etc.
   c. School history from cumulative records, test results, health card, physical record, report cards, etc.

3. Problem Diagnosis
   a. Summarization and interpretation of data
   b. Analyzation of factors and symptoms
   c. Substantiation of results by cross-sectioning

4. Remedial Therapy
   a. Preparation of a program of remediation
   b. Recording of results
   c. Evaluation of the program.

Correction of Difficulty

As indicated previously, the causes of disability are multiple and a complete list would approach infinity in number. It is possible, however, to approach the more commonly encountered difficulties in a general way, keeping in mind that the basis for remediation is knowledge of caused factors. After studying a child and his reading, utilizing the steps outlined earlier, the teacher should be prepared to suggest a course of action to the child. After all, the purpose of remedial reading is to restore the child's confidence in himself as a user of the reading process.

Many readers have reading disabilities because of hindrances foreign to the reading process and the removal of these clears the road to restored confidence. Vision, for example, is often a problem, particularly at the intermediate level, and the referral of the child to a competent specialist may remove this block. Other health and physical impairments can be removed with proper attention. Emotional and home environment disturbances also must be referred to the specialist, since remedial efforts in these areas are beyond the classroom teacher. When these nonreading hindrances are removed, the teacher then embarks upon a therapy program, taking the child at his present achievement and working patiently for improvement.

There are, however, some major areas in reading that, for one reason or another, may have proven to be stumbling blocks. When diagnosis reveals these reading process faults, the teacher of reading must accept the responsibility for remediation as her own and proceed with acceptable technique. Among the reading faults likely to be encountered are the following.

Vocabulary. A limited vocabulary is often the primary source of a child's difficulty in reading. Perhaps he did not have the essential experiences so necessary as background for mastering word meaning, or perhaps he did not receive competent instruction in the skills of word identification. This problem can be attacked in many ways, depending upon the particular need and background of the problem. Steps for building vocabulary strength, not necessarily in order, might include:

1. Analyze vocabulary deficiencies of the child by formal or informal testing.
2. Restore confidence and stimulate interest in learning new words (it can be fun, even for the child with a handicap).
3. Independence in word attack, including skills of phonetic and structural analysis, should be reviewed and strengthened.
4. Sources of words might be studied and unusual, exciting word games played.
5. To become a part of a child's vocabulary, words must be used and the child's communication skills, including speaking, listening, and writing, should receive attention.

Comprehension. Various levels of comprehension are attained at different grades. By the intermediate grades, the child should be able to estimate character, guess at motives with logic, and reason with implied meanings. Children with reading disability are not likely to have mastered such delicate and deep processes and will need much help in developing insight into the printed word. Many children fail to grasp the essential factor that accompanies successful reading, namely the *purpose* in reading a selection. Procedures for strengthening comprehension are much the same as those discussed in previous chapters but particular emphasis must be placed upon:

1. Reading for information, and with a self-oriented purpose.
2. Evaluation of all reading done, including outside reading; the child must be given practice in asking himself if the purpose for the reading has been fulfilled.
3. Readiness for the selection must be assured, as emphasized in Chapter 1.

Speed of Reading. There are many reasons that a child becomes a slow reader. Some material *should* be read slowly, and savored much as one savors any delightful and sensual experience. If this slowness prevails in all reading, however, comprehension becomes a problem. Common reasons for slow reading include:

1. Vocalization. Often this problem can be removed with a simple explanation and change of habit. Removal of strain and tension will also help.

2. Eye movements. Assuming that any physical limitations have been removed, the teacher will prescribe drill to reduce the number of fixations per line and provide material to develop steady reading. Exercises for eye movement drill are listed in many remedial reading manuals and can be prescribed by the specialist if severe difficulties exist. In many instances, faulty eye habits that have been built up as the result of too difficult material tend to correct themselves as speed and ability increase.

3. Word reading. Difficulty with this hindrance usually can be overcome by drill with phrase cards or the tachistoscope.

Corrective Materials

The availability of a tremendously wide variety and range of materials is essential to any sound reading program and an absolute necessity when the remedial program is included. Since the children to whom the remedial reading program is addressed have incurred their disability while using conventional classroom material, their needs will be even greater if new material is presented. The more reading material available the easier will be the task of the teacher to restore confidence and excite interest.

Selection of Materials. Criteria for the suitability of remedial materials might include:

1. The material must be of a type that will aid in correcting the particular faults found. Many exercises and books are designed to correct specific items such as slow reading, lack of comprehension, poor vocabulary, etc.

2. The material must be simple enough for the child to read easily and with understanding. For example, a retarded reader with a fifth grade reading age would never be given sixth grade material, regardless of actual grade placement. In addition any books used in remedial instruction should not have been used before by the child in an instructional situation.

3. The material must be of interest to the child. No child will read, with an attempt to improve, any material that he does not like, take an interest in, or understand.

4. The material should be selected so as to allow the slow reader to develop with the class whenever possible, and to provide him with content so that he too can make contributions. It should be correlated with the theme of the other classwork.

5. The material must be readily available to the teacher and to the child whenever it is needed.

Sources of Materials. There is really no limit as to the number and sources of materials that are available to the teacher today. The creative teacher will find material for his remedial work to be of many types, including:

1. Basic readers and textbooks. Use of materials such as these is limited somewhat because they are graded in difficulty and interest and have often been encountered by the child previously. A little time spent in searching for suitable stories will, however, prove to be of value.

2. Special exercises and workbooks. Various types of commercial materials under this heading are available. The teacher must select these in terms of appropriate interest and need.

3. Classroom and school library collections. A knowledge of what books are available in all categories is essential. The fortunate teacher will receive much help from the librarian in her school.

4. Magazines and newspapers. Current events material, classroom papers, and daily papers are sources of reading practice material and stimulating activities.

5. Visual aids. Any visual can be used to stimulate interest and to aid in instruction. Films, filmstrips, pictures, charts, slides, etc., can all be of value. Such media also do much to stimulate interest in literature.

Sources of Book Lists

Association for Childhod Education International. *Bibliography of Books for Children*. Washington, D. C.: Revised Annually.

Child Study Association. *The Children's Bookshelf*. New York: Bantam Books, 1962.

Fenner, Phyllis. *The Proof of the Pudding: What Children Read*. New York: John Day Co., 1957.

Frank, Josette. *Your Child's Reading Today*. Garden City, New York: Doubleday and Co., Inc., 1960.

Hill, Margaret Keyser. *A Bibliography of Reading Lists for Retarded Readers*. State University of Iowa Extension Bulletin No. 37. Iowa City: State University of Iowa, 1953.

Hunt, J. T. "Easy and Interesting Fiction for the Handicapped Reader." *High School Journal*, 39. April, 1956.

Larrick, Nancy. *A Parent's Guide to Children's Reading*. Garden City, New York: Doubleday and Co., Inc., 1958.

National Council of Teachers of English. *Best Books for Children*. New York: R. R. Bowker Co., 1962.

Neese, Dora J. *A Survey of Corrective and Remedial Reading Materials*. Billings, Montana: Eastern Montana College of Education.

Strang, Ruth, Phelps, Ethlyne, and Withrow, Dorothy. *Gateways to Readable Books*. New York: H. W. Wilson Co., 1958.

Questions for Class Discussion

1. What constitutes disability in reading?
2. What are the valid bases upon which cases in need of remedial training can be identified?
3. What relationships between measures of reading achievement and mental maturity should be considered in selecting the pupil in need of special instruction?
4. What constitutes the suitability of remedial materials in relation to the results of diagnostic measures used?
5. How can an individual classroom teacher best handle remedial pupils?

6. What can be done to bring about a concentrated attack by a school faculty to eliminate the need for remedial reading?

ACTIVITIES FOR FURTHER STUDY

1. Outline the steps to take in identifying the pupil in need of corrective instruction in reading, listing your selection of tests and check lists.
2. Select a child and prepare a complete case study, following the form suggested in this chapter.
3. Make a study of the children who teachers in your school regard as severe reading problems and see if you can isolate any particular pattern that might contribute to this disability.

SELECTED READINGS

AUSTIN, MARY C., BUSH, CLIFFORD L., AND HUEBNER, MILDRED H. *Reading Evaluation: Appraisal Techniques for School and Classroom.* New York: The Ronald Press Co., 1961.

BARBE, WALTER B. *Educator's Guide to Personalized Reading Instruction.* Englewood Cliffs, New Jersey: Prentice-Hall, Inc., 1960.

BLAIR, GLENN M. *Diagnostic and Remedial Teaching.* New York: The Macmillan Co., 1956.

BOND, GEORGE W. "Meeting the Needs of Children with Reading Disabilities," *Educational Administration and Supervision,* XXXVIII (1952), 33-34.

BOND, GUY L., AND TINKER, MILES A. *Reading Difficulties: Their Diagnosis and Correction.* New York: Appleton-Century-Crofts, Inc., 1957.

BROOKS, HAROLD F., AND BRUCE, PAUL. "The Characteristics of Good and Poor Readers as Disclosed by the Wechsler Intelligence Scale for Children," *Journal of Educational Psychology,* 46:488-493, December, 1955.

DRISCOLL, GERTRUDE P. *How to Study the Behavior of Children.* New York: Bureau of Publications, Columbia University, 1936.

EDWARDS, L., AND DOLCH, E. W. "Introducing a Remedial Program," *Elementary English,* XXXII (1955), 36-43.

HARRIS, ALBERT J. *How to Increase Reading Ability,* 4th ed. New York: David McKay Company, Inc., 1961.

HARRIS, JANET D. "The Specialized Remedial-Reading Program versus the Remedial-Reading Program in the Classroom," *Elementary School Journal,* (1955), 160-66.

KEPHART, NEWELL. *The Slow Learner in the Classroom.* Columbus, Ohio: Charles E. Merrill Books, Inc., 1959.

KOTTMEYER, WILLIAM. *Teachers Guide for Remedial Reading.* St. Louis: Welster Publishing Co., 1959.

ODELL, C. W. *How to Improve Classroom Testing.* Dubuque, Iowa: Wm. C. Brown and Company, 1953.

ROBINSON, HELEN M. *Why Pupils Fail in Reading.* Chicago: University of Chicago Press, 1946.

ROBY, D. L. "Learning About Pupils: Non-test Tools and Their Uses," *Teachers College Record,* 31:65-66, December, 1959.

SPACHE, GEORGE D. *Good Reading for Poor Readers.* Champaign, Illinois: Garrand Press, 1959.

SPACHE, GEORGE D. "Diagnosis of Reading Problems in the Classroom," *Education Digest,* 26:47-49, November, 1960.

THOMAS, R. MURRAY. *Judging Pupil Progress.* New York: Longmans, Green and Co., Inc., 1960.

VERNON, PHILIP E. *The Measurement of Abilities.* New York: Philosophical Library, Inc., 1961.

WOOLF, MAURICE D., AND WOOLF, JEANNE A. *Remedial Reading Teaching and Treatment.* New York: McGraw-Hill Book Co., Inc., 1957.

APPENDIX | A

Skill Building Materials for Intermediate Grades

American Book Company:
Adventures in Dictionary Land by E. E. Lewis and others
Word Quiz
American Education Publications:
Current Events
Read
Barnell Loft, Ltd.
Locating the Answer
Using the Context
Working with Sounds
Getting the Facts
Bobbs Merrill Company, Inc.:
Developmental Reading Text-Workbook Series, William H. Burton and others.
Bureau of Publications:
Practice Exercises in Reading by A. I. Gates and C. C. Peardon
Standard Test Lessons in Reading by William A. McCall and Lelaah Mae Crabbs
Continental Press, Inc.:
Reading-Thinking Skills by Ethel S. Maney
Education Center:
Read-Study Practice Books by Eleanor M. Johnson
Phonics and Word Power Practice Books
My Weekly Reader
Educational Developmental Laboratories, Inc.:
Study Skills Library
EDL Word Watching
Educators Publishing Service:
Vocabulary Builder Service
Word Attack Manual by Josephine Rudd
Follett Publishing Company:
The Botel Reading Inventory by Morton Botel
Globe Book Company:
Effective Reading by Lawrence H. Feigenbaum
Successful Reading by Lawrence H. Feigenbaum
C. S. Hammond and Company:
Words are Important by H. C. Hardwick
Harcourt, Brace and World, Inc.:
Harbrace Vocabulary Workshop by Paul Schweitzer and Donald W. Lee
Word Analysis Practice by Donald D. Durrell and others
Laidlaw Brothers:
Developing Reading Skills by Neal and Foster

109

Macmillan Publishing Company:
The Macmillan Reading Spectrum
Aviation Series Books
Core Aviation Readers by Mariam B. Huber, Frank S. Salisbury and
    Arthur I. Gates
Sports Readers

Charles E. Merrill, Inc.:
Diagnostic Reading Workbooks by Eleanor M. Johnson
New Reading Skilltext Series by Eleanor M. Johnson
Reading Adventures Series

Reader's Digest Services, Inc.:
Reader's Digest Reading Skill Builders

Science Research Associates, Inc.:
Elementary Reading Laboratory
SRA Reading Laboratory IIc
Reading for Understanding
Pilot Library IIc
Better Reading Books by Elizabeth Simpson

Scott Foresman and Company:
Basic Reading Skills for Junior High School by William S. Gray

Steck Company:
The Reading Essentials Series by Ullin W. Leavell
New Goals in Reading

Harr Wagner Publishing Company:
Morgan Bay Mystery Series by John and Nancy Rambeau
Jim Forest Readers by John and Nancy Rambeau
The Deep Sea Adventure Series by Frances Berres, James C. Coleman,
    William S. Briscoe and Frank M. Hewett

Webster Publishing Company:
New Practice Readers by Clarence B. Stone and others

APPENDIX | B

Publishers and Addresses

American Book Company, 55 Fifth Avenue, New York 3, N. Y.
American Education Publications, Columbus 16, Ohio
Barnell Loft, Ltd., Rockville Centre, New York
Bobbs-Merrill Co., Inc., 730 N. Meridian Street, Indianapolis 7, Indiana
Bureau of Publications, Columbia University, New York 27, N. Y.
Continental Press, Inc., Elizabethtown, Pa.
Education Center, Columbus, Ohio
Educational Developmental Laboratories, Inc., Huntington, N. Y.
Educators Publishing Service, 301 Vassar Street, Cambridge, Mass.
Follett Publishing Company, 1010 W. Washington Blvd., Chicago, Ill.
Globe Book Company, 175 Fifth Avenue, New York 10, N. Y.
C. S. Hammond & Co., Inc., 521 Fifth Avenue, New York 17, N. Y.
Harcourt, Brace and Co., Inc., 750 3rd Avenue, New York 17, N. Y.
Laidlaw Brothers, 36 Chatham Road, Summit, New Jersey
Macmillan Co., 60 Fifth Avenue, New York 11, New York
Charles E. Merrill Co., Inc., 1300 Alum Creek Drive, Columbus 16, Ohio
Reader's Digest Educational Dept., Pleasantville, N. Y.
Science Research Associates, Inc., 259 East Erie Street, Chicago 11, Ill.
Steck Company Publishers, Box 16, Austin 61, Texas
Harr Wagner Publishing Co., 609 Mission St., San Francisco 5, Calif.
Webster Publishing Co., 1808 Washington Avenue, St. Louis 3, Mo.